GREAT LEADER
GREAT TEACHER

RECOVERING THE BIBLICAL
VISION FOR LEADERSHIP

GARY BREDFELDT

MOODY PUBLIS
CHICAGO

All Scripture quotations, unless otherwise indicated, are taken from the *Holy Bible, New International Version®*. NIV®. Copyright © 1973, 1978, 1984 by International Bible Society. Used by permission of Zondervan Publishing House. All rights reserved.

Scripture quotations marked NASB are taken from the *New American Standard Bible®*, © Copyright by The Lockman Foundation 1960, 1962, 1963, 1968, 1971, 1972, 1973, 1975, 1977, 1995. Used by permission.

Scripture quotations marked NKJV are taken from The New King James Version, Thomas Nelson Publishers. Copyright © 1982 by Thomas Nelson Inc. Used by permission. All rights reserved.

ISBN: 0-8024-1147-9
ISBN-13: 978-0-8024-1147-1

Cover Design: Paetzold Associates
Cover Image: Corbis
Interior Design: Ragont Design
Editor: Pam Pugh

Library of Congress Cataloging-in-Publication Data

Bredfeldt, Gary J.
  Great leader great teacher : recovering the biblical vision for leadership/Gary Bredfeldt.
    p. cm.
Includes bibliographical references.
ISBN-13: 978-0-8024-1147-1
1. Christian leadership. I. Title.
BV652.1.B73 2006
253--dc22

2006015954

We hope you enjoy this book from Moody Publishers. Our goal is to provide high-quality, thought-provoking books and products that connect truth to your real needs and challenges. For more information on other books and products written and produced from a biblical perspective, go to www.moodypublishers.com or write to:

Moody Publishers
820 N. LaSalle Boulevard
Chicago, IL 60610

1 3 5 7 9 10 8 6 4 2

Printed in the United States of America

To those men and women who, each week, in churches both large and small, open the Word of God and teach its life-changing message.

To those pastors of smaller churches who, from time to time, compare themselves to others leading larger ministries—May this book encourage you as you teach God's Word and as you shepherd the flock God has put under your care. Your leadership is not measured in terms of baptisms, buildings, or budgets, but in terms of your faithfulness in the teaching of the Word of God.

And to my family, who continue to encourage me and support me in the process of writing. Marlene, Lynne, Stephen, Michael, and Amy, you are God's gift to me.

CONTENTS

FOREWORD
by R. Albert Mohler, Jr.

IN today's church, leadership has become something of an obsession. In one sense, this is almost natural and necessary, as leadership is absolutely essential to any organization, including the church. Nevertheless, the obsessive interest in leadership has served to distract the church from the nature of leadership as revealed in the Scripture. Instead, Christians have been tempted to draw leadership models from the worlds of finance, commerce, politics, and even sports—instead of looking for a distinctly Christian understanding of leadership as revealed in the Scriptures.

Without doubt, the church should be concerned with issues such as efficiency, effectiveness, and influence. Nevertheless, the biblical standard of leadership transcends all of these concerns. Genuine Christian leadership is never reducible to matters of pragmatic theory, managerial advice, or social esteem.

In *Great Leader, Great Teacher,* Gary Bredfeldt writes with passion, vision, and genuine Christian insight. He understands the nature of biblical leadership and points the church toward models that transcend the secular ideal that has become the fascination in far too many circles. In this book, professor Bredfeldt combines what might be called theory and practice in developing a comprehensive model of the leader as a teacher. This is a vitally important truth that must be recovered in this generation—that the essence of Christian leadership is teaching. This truth was especially evident in the model of Jesus with His disciples, and it is also the paradigm of leadership as found in the New Testament church. First and foremost, the Christian leader is one who teaches the Word of God. And the recovery of this sense of Christian leadership is absolutely necessary for the church's health in this generation.

Gary Bredfeldt is a skilled teacher who leads by example. In this book, he writes from a wealth of experience in the local church and in college and seminary teaching. He is a man of deep passion, great conviction, and keen insight. In *Great Leader, Great Teacher,* Gary Bredfeldt points us all to a higher standard of leadership and to faithfulness in teaching the word of God. This alone makes this book invaluable for today's church.

INTRODUCTION

BEHIND this book is a conviction that God's most common means of leading His people is through those who teach His people.

Much has been written on the subject of leadership. Topics such as leading change, casting vision, strategic planning, and building effective teams fill books. They are helpful and valuable resources to those who seek to lead any organization. In fact, I use them in the classes I teach to doctoral students at Southern Baptist Theological Seminary in Louisville, Kentucky. But one aspect of leadership seems to have been overlooked in most of these works—the role of teaching in the practice of leadership. This book seeks to address that facet of leadership, especially as it relates to leading God's people in and through the local church.

When the word *leader* is mentioned, often our minds go to persons of rank who direct the affairs of organizations or to the entrepreneurs who cast the vision for new and dynamic ventures. We sometimes picture athletic coaches or military generals, corporate CEOs and megachurch pastors. Those certainly all qualify as leaders, but I want you to picture another kind of leader—the leader-teacher. I am convinced that the most powerful leaders among us are the teachers among us.

I recently heard the story of a woman who attended her twenty-year high school reunion. While there she bumped into her art teacher from her freshman year. The woman proceeded to tell the art teacher about how inspirational his teaching was during her high school years. She informed him that she had determined to go to college to study art as a result of his encouragement. She went on to tell her high school teacher that she was an art professor at a large and prestigious state university. At the end of the evening's reunion activities, the high school teacher looked one more time for his former student. He again shook her hand and said, "Thank you for saying those nice things about my teaching. You've really made my day."

"You're welcome," replied the woman, with a tear sliding down her cheek. "But let me thank you—you've made my life!"

Teachers are powerful leaders. And among those teachers who lead most effectively are those who teach God's Word with accuracy, enthusiasm, and faithfulness.

Charles Haddon Spurgeon has been called the Prince of Preachers, and his ministry at London's Metropolitan Tabernacle in the mid-to-late 1800s was legendary. Between 1863 and 1891, the year of Spurgeon's death, the Tabernacle averaged over five thousand in weekly attendance. Timothy George writes that, "Spurgeon was a mega-church pastor before megachurches were cool."[1]

While Spurgeon is well-known as a leader-teacher, another lesser-known leader-teacher was also having an impact at the very same church during the very same time frame. Her name was Lavinia Bartlett.

Mrs. Lavinia Bartlett was a woman's Bible class teacher at the Metropolitan Tabernacle. In 1859, Mrs. Bartlett began her class with just three young women. During the course of the first month together, her class grew to fourteen ladies in attendance. Her class grew steadily over the next six months when it reached six hundred attendees. It is estimated that during her fourteen years of teaching, Mrs. Bartlett added over one thousand people to the ministry of the Tabernacle.

What is more, most of this growth was conversion growth. These were not people jumping from church to church; these were new believers brought to Christ by this faithful teacher of the Word of God. These were unchurched women with many concerns and problems. In response, she opened her home and her heart to those she taught. So powerful was her teaching ministry that Spurgeon himself called her home a "house of mercy."

But Mrs. Bartlett did not simply reach people and convert them to Christianity—she discipled them as well. Mrs. Bartlett was concerned that those she taught would grow in their faith and would themselves be mobilized for ministry. Spurgeon once said of Mrs. Bartlett, "She trained her disciples into a band of laborers, and kept them all at it to the utmost of their abilities." The result was a multiplication of her leading-teaching ministry as her class produced missionaries and teachers. In addition, the class contributed to the training of pastors through their financial generosity.[2]

Mrs. Bartlett was a leader-teacher. She shaped lives through her teaching ministry and in the process gave leadership to the church. This book is about leading through the ministry of teaching.

Chapter One

ACHIEVING MAXIMUM LEADERSHIP:
TEACHING THE WORD

And the things you have heard me say in the presence of many witnesses entrust to reliable men who will also be qualified to teach others.

—2 Timothy 2:2

THE greatest of leaders among us are not powerful senior executives, commanding military strategists, celebrated athletic coaches, or respected political figures. No, the greatest leaders among us are the great teachers among us. In a hundred ways and in a hundred different arenas, great teachers, every day, influence through their passion, their character, and their words. Teachers shape, challenge, and change people, and in doing so, they lead. Great teachers are leaders, and conversely, great leaders must be teachers.

Defining leadership is an elusive thing. Is leadership a position? Is it a person? Is it a process? Maybe it is power and influence. And once we define it, what role should one play in exercising it? Should one take the role of a commander, a coach, colleague, or simply co-laboring community member?

The confusion over how to define leadership grows out of the complexity of leadership itself. The nature of leadership differs from situation to situation. What is required of a leader on the battlefield is quite different from what is required on the ball field or mission field. Leadership is not a one-size-fits-all formula. The nature of leadership shifts with the context, the followers, the task, and even the leader himself or herself. What is clear is that leadership is dynamic and requires openness and flexibility on the part of those who must exercise leadership in their work, ministry, or family contexts.

In recent days, new winds have been blowing in the leadership realm. There are calls to abandon "hierarchal" and "heroic" models of leadership in favor of "authentic," "transformational," and "post-heroic" models of leadership.[1] Even in the church, new voices are being heard that call for a departure from a "leadership of ideology" to a "values-driven" leadership and from a "leadership of controlling hierarchy" to a leadership of "empowered networks of Christ followers."[2] Out is the management emphasis of strategic planning and in is a new emphasis on learning, development, and mutuality where authority is replaced with authenticity. Today, leadership has become distributed and decentralized and less vested in a single individual at the top of the organizational pyramid. The question is this: Is that a positive thing or a negative thing for the church? Are we heading the right direction, or could we simply be watching a pendulum reaction to the marketing approaches to leadership popular in the 1980s and '90s?

Authors like Peter Senge[3] from a business perspective and Eddie Gibbs from a church perspective are challenging the very foundations of our thinking about leadership. Immersed in the currents of contemporary culture, these authors call leaders to a postmodern approach to the task of leadership where leaders no longer have the answers, but instead create a climate where followers are empowered, collaborative, and freed to pursue shared goals in their own way.

Those, like me, who embrace a firm, conservative commitment to the ultimate authority of Scripture as the Word of God are concerned. We wonder, are these new winds threatening to blow the church off course? And if the church follows the powerful currents of postmodern culture when it comes to leadership, does it run the risk of losing its rudder altogether for the sake of remaining contemporary and responsive to cultural shifts? If the relativism and experience-driven standards of culture are embraced, it seems likely that the church will simply be pushed along and become indistinguishable from the world to which it is to be a witness.

This book is a call to leadership by the Book, that is, the Bible. It is an exploration of the most fundamental aspect of biblical leadership: the teaching of the Word of God as the life-changing power of God. It reflects an unabashed commitment to Scripture as propositional truth, often embedded in the communication vehicle of story. At the most basic core of biblical leadership is one indispensable, unchanging function of the Christian leader—the task of teaching God's Word with clarity, in its original context, and in a way that is relevant to those whose hearts are open to hear. This is leadership in its simplest, most distilled form. The biblical leader is first and foremost a Bible teacher, and the people of God are a distinctive teaching-learning community where the principles of business leadership may not always apply.

LEADING GOD'S TEACHING-LEARNING COMMUNITY

The National Aeronautics and Space Administration (NASA) is an example of the best and worst in leadership. The amazing rescue of *Apollo 13* is a testament of human ingenuity and creativity, a wonderful expression of teamwork at its best. *Apollo 13* left its launching pad on April 11, 1970 bound for the moon. But just a day into the mission an explosion occurred that damaged the spacecraft. The damage was severe, making the command module useless and causing life-supporting oxygen to vent from the side of the craft. With no options but to abort the mission to the moon, plans turned to a rescue. The challenge was to figure out a way to use the lunar lander as a lifeboat in order to get the spacecraft and its crew safely to Earth. The task required considerable improvisation by the crew and the support workers on Earth. In a matchless feat of teamwork and leadership, the rescue succeeded and all returned safely. The astronauts and the ground crew engaged together in a tremendously complex learning activity. *Apollo 13* was an example of a learning organization at its best.

Not all of the stories that surround NASA have had such a positive ending. The story of the *Challenger* disaster on January 28, 1986, stands as a worst-case illustration of bureaucracy and traditional management practices. Engineers from the Grumman Corporation, manufacturer of the O-rings that sealed the solid-fuel booster rockets, tried to tell NASA officials that the O-rings might fail due to extremely cold conditions the night before the launch. The management at NASA did not want to learn about the problem because it might threaten to stop the mission. A delay would have placed the program in jeopardy and damaged the careers and reputations of those in leadership. In fact, when one engineer tried to communicate the problem, he was pressured to drop the issue and support the project. This nonlearning, nonteaching, group-think environment had the effect of lowering the combined IQ of the entire team. Lack of coordinated effort, a lack of unified energy, and a failure to function as a teaching-learning organization directly resulted in the catastrophic explosion of the shuttle just after liftoff.[4] It was a tragedy that might have been avoidable had the NASA leadership valued learning and teaching over schedules and politics. But it is easy to get priorities mixed up when measurements of success and failure are quantified in statistics and personal career advancement. This is an error in perspective all too familiar to those who lead the church as well.

The church is fundamentally a teaching-learning organization. Its future depends on the effectiveness of its leaders and members as they function as both teachers and learners. Visionary planning is important, mission statements are useful, and purpose-driven strategies can be invaluable in growing the church numerically, but if, in the process, the central task of teaching is lost, the church will have paid a steep price for its material successes. For in the end, the goal is not numerical growth, but mature followers of Jesus Christ. Paul put it clearly when he said, "We proclaim him, admonishing and teaching everyone with all wisdom, so that we may present everyone perfect in Christ. To this end I labor, struggling with all his energy, which so powerfully works in me" (Colossians 1:28–29). The word *perfect* does not mean *flawless*; it means *mature*. Paul understood the "end" or goal to be the maturity of God's people.

Spiritual maturity is promoted by a commitment to teaching the Word of God. Spiritual growth is not instantaneous and it is not easily measured. It is slow. It is hard work. It is time-consuming. Nevertheless, it is the measure of an effective church. Spiritual maturity is a process that begins with the teaching of the simple gospel and continues on to the more difficult truths of the Word of God. The author of Hebrews links teaching to this maturational process and even makes the need to teach a prerequisite to spiritual maturity.

> We have much to say about this, but it is hard to explain because you are slow to learn. In fact, though by this time you ought to be teachers, you need someone to teach you the elementary truths of God's word all over again. You need milk, not solid food! Anyone who lives on milk, being still an infant, is not acquainted with the teaching about righteousness. But solid food is for the mature, who by constant use have trained themselves to distinguish good from evil.
>
> Therefore let us leave the elementary teachings about Christ and go on to maturity, not laying again the foundation of repentance from acts that lead to death, and of faith in God, instruction about baptisms, the laying on of hands, the resurrection of the dead, and eternal judgment. (Hebrews 5:11–6:2)

By its nature, the church must be a teaching-learning organization. But the church is even more than that. It is a living organism, and as such, it can both grow and learn. For these purposes, God gives the church leaders to communicate the Word of God and to equip the people of

God. Paul puts it this way in Ephesians 4:11–16.

> It was he who gave some to be apostles, some to be prophets, some to be evangelists, and some to be pastors and teachers, to prepare God's people for works of service, so that the body of Christ may be built up until we all reach unity in the faith and in the knowledge of the Son of God and become mature, attaining to the whole measure of the fullness of Christ.
>
> Then we will no longer be infants, tossed back and forth by the waves, and blown here and there by every wind of teaching and by the cunning and craftiness of men in their deceitful scheming. Instead, speaking the truth in love, we will in all things grow up into him who is the Head, that is, Christ. From him the whole body, joined and held together by every supporting ligament, grows and builds itself up in love, as each part does its work.

Notice the leaders listed in this passage—apostles, prophets, evangelists, and pastor-teachers. What quality do they share in common? It is their role as teacher-leaders. They are called to "speak the truth in love." All of these gifted persons are communicators of the Word of God. *The most powerful means of leading the people of God is by teaching them the Word of God.* Through its teacher-leaders, truth is spoken in love and thus prepares God's people for works of service that lead to the growth and maturation of the body of Christ. That maturity is marked by increased unity, knowledge, and Christlikeness, as well as a lessening vulnerability to the deceptions of false teachers.

Achieving Maximum Leadership

In a day when access to highly researched leadership theories abounds, many of which offer valuable insights into organizational leadership, Christian leaders need to recognize that the most potent principle of leadership is fundamentally a biblical principle. *Maximum leadership is achieved through great teaching.* For the Christian leader, there is no more basic principle of leadership. Those who teach and teach well are truly the greatest of leaders. Teachers are great leaders for three basic reasons—they have great influence, they bring about great change, and they can invoke the highest levels of follower development.

Teachers Have Great Influence

Leadership has most often been defined in a single word—*influence.*[5] That is to say, leaders are those individuals who, through their personality, position, or power, shape the outlook and future of others. Whether positively or not, leaders influence others. If that is true, then certainly teachers are leaders, for teachers influence students cognitively, affectively, and behaviorally. Moreover, it could be argued that the greatest of leaders are the teachers among us and that any leader who truly desires to have an enduring impact must learn to teach.

Teachers influence through the power of ideas and the process of modeling. One teacher can change a single life or spark a great movement. The impact of just one teacher can spread exponentially. Combine the impassioned words of a teacher with a credible life, and social, political, and even spiritual change can spread like a California wildfire consuming a hillside.

Some of the most influential teachers are those who labor faithfully, often unacknowledged, in classrooms, Sunday schools, club ministries, and mentoring programs across the nation.

Freida J. Riley was a science and math teacher at Big Creek High School in Coalwood, West Virginia. Coalwood was a place of limited opportunities and very clear expectations. The norm for the boys of Coalwood was to start working at the mine just after high school. But Freida Riley could not accept that norm. As a person of faith, Miss Riley considered it her calling to inspire her students to overcome the confines of their era and environment. She taught so that each student would aspire to fulfill their dreams of doing great things. She did this despite suffering with Hodgkin's disease through most of her teaching career. Miss Riley died at the age of thirty-one, dearly loved by her students. But she died having left a lasting impact on her students. Miss Riley was a leader because she taught with skill and influence.

The following memorial tribute is taken from the Big Creek High School yearbook[6] after her death in 1969:

> Big Creek was deeply saddened by the death of Miss Freida Riley August 5, 1969. She had taught math, chemistry, and physics here for ten years. Her life should not be measured in terms of years, however; though brief, her life was one of accomplishment. She strived for and achieved excellence as a student, teacher, and person.
>
> Miss Riley ranked first in the 1955 graduating class of Big Creek and first in the 1959 class of Concord College. She continued her studies in math at Ohio State University and West Virginia University. As a teacher, Miss Riley impressed and inspired her students with continued success.
>
> Former students have much praise for her. "Miss Riley taught because she wanted her students to learn." "She made people want to learn; she helped one understand the value of education." "In all my years of education I have met very few teachers her equal in their devotion to their students."

If leadership is influence, then Miss Riley was a leader and a powerful leader at that. By her words and by her walk, Miss Riley influenced followers. Her students and coworkers were also touched by the warmth of her personality and wrote of her with words like these: "She was a combination of intelligence, wit, compassion, empathy, and love, a rare combination." One graduate, in words any teacher would long to hear, stated that, "I feel that my life has been greatly enriched by having her as a teacher and as a friend." Miss Riley was a great teacher and as such, Miss Riley was a great leader. Her leadership was evidenced by the lives of students she touched as a faithful teacher.

The Rocket Boys grew up in Coalwood and attended Miss Riley's science class at Big Creek High School. Jimmy "O'Dell" Carroll, Roy Lee Cooke, Quentin Wilson, Willie Rose, and Homer Hickam were five boys who dreamed of a life outside of Coalwood. Because of Miss Riley's teaching and encouragement, one of those boys, Homer, envisioned that one day he would be a rocket designer. With great passion, Homer recruited his friends to help him design his first rocket. Seeing their growing interest in rocketry, Miss Riley pushed those boys and motivated them to enter their rocket in the state science fair. Together, against the odds and against enormous obstacles, they won not only the state fair, but the national science fair as well. With the win came a scholarship for each boy to attend college. Their story is captured by Homer Hickam in his book *The Rocket Boys*, which was made into the 1999 film *October Sky*.[7] In the book, Homer describes the support given by his teacher Miss Riley, and how she motivated him and his friends to achieve results beyond what any of them could have expected. Homer, encouraged by a teacher-leader, not only won that science fair and scholarship, he gained the opportunity to pursue his dream. Homer went on to became an aerospace engineer for NASA serving the space shuttle program as a crew trainer.

Homer's story continues to encourage and Miss Riley's teacher-leader sacrifice continues to enrich the lives of many. You see, her students will long remember the influence of a devoted teacher and an inspirational individual. As the final paragraph in that 1969 yearbook read:

> *The greatest tribute that we can give is to emulate the principles by which she lived: a deep faith in God, the courage to face difficulties, a sincere concern for others, the unselfish quality to give of herself, a respect for knowledge, and the desire for excellence.*

By teaching more than chemistry and physics, Miss Riley led the Rocket Boys to a new future. Yes, great teachers are great leaders. But flip the sentence around and you have another true statement: Great leaders are also great teachers. Through the skill of teaching and the communicating of ideas, leaders have an amazing power to promote change. In fact, leaders who effectively teach can engender an entire social movement.

Teachers Can Bring About Great Change

There is a difference between a movement and an organization. One fosters change and the other promotes order. One values transformation; the other values consolidation and conservation of gains. Both are needed, but each calls for a different kind of leadership. Movements are about change and are led by visionary teachers and great communicators. Organizations are about structure and solidifying change and are led by managers and executives. Movements grow from great ideas communicated by those who hold them passionately. Organizations grow out of strategic plans devised and implemented by managerial professionals. Movements are chaotic, energetic, and at times ill defined. Organizations are stable, institutional, and corporate.

Movements operate at the cutting edge, while organizations lag somewhere behind—how far behind depends on the organizational leadership. Organizations can promote movements within, but only if leaders recognize a need for change. If the status quo is the goal, organizations will isolate, marginalize, and even force out promoters of new ideas and communicators of a new vision for the future. Such organizations are destined to die as new movements overpower them, and new organizations and structures arise in their place.

The civil rights movement is an example of this principle at work. In its earliest days, its leaders were teachers who taught its foundational principles through both action and word. Rosa Parks, the African-American woman whose act of courage in refusing to relinquish her bus seat to a white man, inspired the wheels of the civil rights movement to keep turning. In her action, she taught that equality is practical, not theoretical. Her willingness to be arrested, stand trial, and even face jail taught a transforming message through role modeling and civil disobedience. It was a message that the NAACP struggled to communicate through political and corporate processes. It took an individual willing to teach through her actions to begin a movement and bring change.

Similarly, the civil rights movement was led by a teacher whose words fostered change. Dr. Martin Luther King Jr. taught a vision for a different kind of America. His message was captured in his renowned "I have a dream" speech. The following excerpt from this engaging speech capture its central message, and the central teaching of the civil rights movement's teacher-leader.

> *I say to you today, my friends, so even though we face the difficulties of today and tomorrow, I still have a dream. It is a dream deeply rooted in the American dream.*
>
> *I have a dream that one day this nation will rise up and live out the true meaning of its creed: "We hold these truths to be self-evident: that all men are created equal."*
>
> *I have a dream that one day on the red hills of Georgia the sons of former slaves and the sons of former slave owners will be able to sit down together at the table of brotherhood.*
>
> *I have a dream that one day even the state of Mississippi, a state sweltering with the heat of injustice . . . [and] oppression, will be transformed into an oasis of freedom and justice.*
>
> *I have a dream that my four children will one day live in a nation where they will not be judged by the color of their skin but by the content of their character.*
>
> *I have a dream today.*[8]

Dr. King used the power of ideas to bring social change. Once released, ideas can lead movements whose energy brings deep and lasting change. However, change wrought by the power of an idea is not without its detractors. Teachers who challenge established thought or institutions are often disliked or worse. In fact, in the process of waking up an organization with the power of truth, teacher-leaders will find that their ideas are threatening for some. While truth does free, it can also be resisted. Why? Because truth brings followers face-to-face with reality. Resistance to change is one of the most difficult challenges a leader will face. Teacher-leaders will often pay a price to make a difference, but leadership is not a popularity contest. Leadership is not for the fainthearted. Leaders who seek to lead through the power of teaching ideas will have those ideas challenged. Sometimes the challenge will come directly and publicly, and sometimes more subtly through the politics of an entrenched bureaucracy.

An event in my own experience as a teacher-leader required that I pay a price for teaching and speaking truth in an effort to bring change. On one occasion, both popularity and political expedience encouraged me to look the other way in a situation that was blatantly unethical. Fortunately, by God's grace and strength, I did not yield to the pressure and found myself speaking the truth and standing my ground. In a respectful way, I had to state why I could not take the politically correct path and why I favored the path of ethical integrity. At the time, my words and actions were not well received. To this day, it probably cost me some favor with certain people; but in the long run, by taking that stand, my ministry was enhanced and respect for my leadership grew. Colleagues who were borderline supporters of my leadership came to welcome my leadership in other contexts because of this stand for truth. The net result was a lesson taught in actions and leadership enacted by teaching the truth. Sometimes, as a teacher-leader you will have to declare that "the emperor has no clothes" and live with the outcome. Truth telling is a form of teaching and a form of leadership.

Teachers are great leaders because they have great influence and because they can bring great organizational and social change. There is still a third reason teachers are great leaders.

Teachers Can Invoke the Highest Levels of Follower Development

Noel M. Tichy, professor at Michigan Business School and director of the school's Global Leadership Partnership, believes that the greatest of leaders are teachers by nature. He believes that they value knowledge and understand its power and therefore, as great leaders, they work to build what he calls *teaching organizations*. Teaching organizations value learning and are concerned that teaching is an explicit goal of the organization. Top leaders in teaching organizations make it their priority to develop people by teaching what they know to others. Tichy states, "Teaching is the most effective means through which a leader can lead."[9] Leaders who understand that principle understand that their primary function as a leader is to create organizational structures where teaching is intentional, explicit, and at the very core of the organization's values.

Tichy identifies teaching as the highest level of leadership because it brings the greatest development in the lives and work of the follower. By focusing on teaching, leaders increase the depth of knowledge in the organization, heighten the level of commitment among organizational members, and generate new leaders who themselves are able to reproduce leaders. He diagrams four leadership levels in the form of a pyramid (see figure 1, page 29).

At the lowest level, leaders *command* their followers. Leaders at this level give mandates and directions with the goal being to command and control their followers' behavior. Followers are given little understanding of the goals and vision behind the mandates. This approach takes the least amount of time on the part of the leader, but also produces the lowest levels of learning, commitment, and leadership development.

At the second level, leaders *tell* their followers their vision, goals, and ideas. Followers are expected to simply adopt the leader's ideas and implement them. Unfortunately, this approach continues to generate a minimal level of commitment, learning, and leadership development.

At the third level, leaders *sell* their followers on their vision and goals. Leaders become motivators who persuade their followers to adopt their ideas. This is often done by allowing some participation in the change process.

Finally, at the highest level, leaders *teach* their followers key concepts, concepts which become the basis for confident action on the part of followers. This results in followers who own those ideas and who develop the means of implementing them. Commitment, learning, and leadership development are the fruit. But teaching takes time and is risky. When teachers entrust ideas to their followers, they empower followers with greater freedom to shape the organization.

The risk of teaching is balanced by the results of teaching. Leaders who risk teaching others and empowering followers with their knowledge and ideas multiply the impact and results of their leadership. Teaching, as the highest level of leadership, brings about the greatest success in achieving the organizational mission.

THE NEED FOR TEACHER-LEADERS

The Great Commission demands that we take the risk of leadership through teaching that empowers followers. In Matthew 28:19–20, Jesus commands us to " . . . go and make disciples of all nations, baptizing them in the name of the Father and of the Son and of the Holy Spirit, and teaching them to obey everything I have commanded you." His command is more than simply a command to "go." It is a command to do something in our act of going—"make disciples." The word *disciple* means *student* or *learner*.

How does one make a disciple? Jesus explains how disciple making is to be accomplished in a two-step process. First, we are to *baptize* persons in the name of the Father and the Son and the Holy Spirit. This is a call to evangelism. Baptism, though not the basis of salvation, is symbolic of a life fully committed to Christ. In the cultural context in which Jesus taught these words, baptism was the means by which a public commitment was declared. Similar to an altar call today, baptism provided the new believer a means to declare the reality of the work of Christ within. Jesus tells His followers that the first step in making disciples is the step of baptism or personal commitment to Christ.

The second step takes us beyond evangelism. It is a call to make disciples by "teaching them to obey everything I have commanded you." As much as the Great Commission is about evangelism, it is also about teaching those we reach. Teaching is at the very heart and center of Christ's commission to the church.

Biblical leadership is a teaching task. Teaching is, in fact, the foundational task of every Christian leader. Paul reminds young pastor Timothy of this fact in 2 Timothy 2:2 when he says, "And the things you have heard me say in the presence of many witnesses entrust to reliable men who will also be qualified to teach others." Paul wanted Timothy to be a teacher. More than that, Paul wanted Timothy to be a teacher of teachers. Timothy needed to understand that the leadership task was greater than one generation training the next generation. It was a charge to "entrust" or empower reliable people who, themselves, would continue the process of leadership development. Four generations of believers are referenced in this short passage—*Paul, Timothy, reliable men,* and *others*. Notice that Timothy is to entrust the message to those who are "qualified to teach." What we have here is a sacred trust or stewardship of the Word of God where leaders, capable of faithful communication, are to equip the next generation. The primary skill of these "next generation leaders" is to be teaching. Why? Because teaching about Jesus, the gospel, and the doctrines of Christ is the focal point of the church's ministry.

Because of this sacred trust, Paul identified the ability to teach as a basic qualification for elders. Paul wrote that, "If anyone sets his heart on being an overseer, he desires a noble task. Now the overseer must be above reproach, the husband of but one wife, temperate, self-controlled, respectable, hospitable, able to teach . . . " (1 Timothy 3:1–2). *Able to teach*—that is the ability to communicate the enduring and unchanging truth of the Word of God to those one is called to lead.

Ideas, expressed in word and action, have the power to make

change—and teachers possess the power of ideas. In James 3, the author warns teachers to be careful in exercising their teaching function. He declares that "Not many of you should presume to be teachers, my brothers, because you know that we who teach will be judged more strictly" (James 3:1). He continues by discussing the power of the tongue.

> Take ships as an example. Although they are so large and are driven by strong winds, they are steered by a very small rudder wherever the pilot wants to go. Likewise the tongue is a small part of the body, but it makes great boasts. Consider what a great forest is set on fire by a small spark. The tongue also is a fire, a world of evil among the parts of the body. It corrupts the whole person, sets the whole course of his life on fire, and is itself set on fire by hell. (James 3:4–6)

Teaching is an enormously powerful means of leading. For good or for bad, the words of a teacher can bring direction or destruction.

The church is at risk. What began so powerfully as a movement has all too often become just an organization. Its leaders have become caretakers of yesterday's gains who surrender the future to movements both good and bad. Here is the fundamental problem. Once the elders of the church, teachers by calling, become chief executive officers rather than teachers, the church is relegated to organizational status. Likewise, when elders simply embrace the culture and its leadership trends, they are set adrift in the cultural currents and lose their ability to speak the Word of God with clarity and authority. The church should be dynamic, cutting-edge, and life-changing in its impact. But this happens only when church leaders teach the Word of God in a relevant manner while retaining a firm commitment to the biblical text and biblical authority.

The work of the church is a work of transformation. It is a work wrought by men and women faithfully teaching the Word of God, which is able to change the very heart with its message. Inspired by the Spirit of God, the Word of God "is useful for teaching, rebuking, correcting and training in righteousness, so that the man of God may be thoroughly equipped for every good work" (2 Timothy 3:16–17).

This book is about achieving maximum leadership. Its principles apply primarily to leadership in the church, but it also applies to leadership in organizations outside the church context. That is because it is about the power of teaching as a leadership skill. Leaders who recognize their function as teachers point followers to a cause far greater than themselves. As Terry Pearce puts it, "Good leaders get people to work for them. Great leaders get people to work for a cause that is greater than any of them—and then for one another in service to that cause."[10] Teachers do just that. Those who learn to teach also learn to maximize their leadership through the act of teaching others.

Figure 1

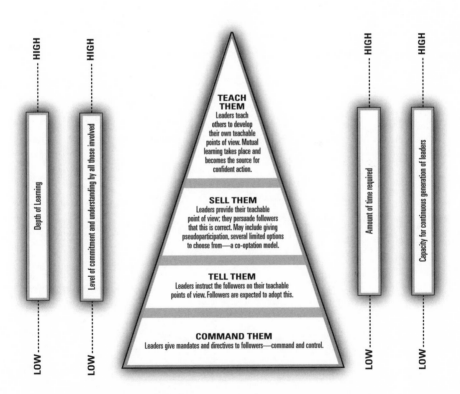

Noel M. Tichy, *The Cycle of Leadership*, Harper Business, 2004, p. 59.

Chapter Two

MISPLACED PRIORITIES:
DISTRACTED BY THE GOOD WHILE MISSING THE BEST

Ezra had set his heart to study the law of the Lord and to practice it, and to teach His statutes and ordinances in Israel.

—Ezra 7:10 NASB

IT is easy to get distracted. Just a moment given to making a cell phone call or correcting a child can lead to a disaster when driving. Distractions have a way of diverting our focus from the essential to the peripheral.

Baseball players know this principle well. Take, for example, the second baseman who is about to turn a routine double play. The momentary distraction of a base runner heading to second causes him to take his eye off the ball and what was to be a simple second-to-short-to-first double play turns into an embarrassing error with a ball scooting between his legs.

Distractions cause us to lose focus and misplay the game before us. This is especially true if you are a ministry leader. Consider the story of a Southern Baptist pastor I once met. He was a student in one of my doctoral courses at Southern Seminary in Louisville. The story is true, though his name has been changed.

A Case Study in Misplaced Priorities

Pastor Brian Hill had a full day planned. It was Wednesday, always a long day. His day was to begin at eight o'clock, when he was scheduled to sit down for coffee with the office staff. They would have a brief devotional together followed by a staff meeting, at which details of upcoming events would be discussed. At nine that morning, he was to meet with the new youth pastor, Mark. Mark was fresh out of seminary and needed a lot of orientation to life on a church staff. Pastor Brian felt it was his responsibility to mentor Mark through his early days of ministry. That meant that he had to make these times together a top priority. At ten, Lance, the church's part-time worship pastor, was supposed to come by and go over the plans for Sunday morning's worship service. Brian had hoped that he would be better prepared for plans for the upcoming service before Lance arrived, but it looked like he would not have much done on his sermon because of the unexpected funeral he had conducted on Tuesday.

Pastor Brian's meeting with Lance took longer than expected. Lance told him that the keyboardist in the worship band had quit. It seems that she had heard that one of the elders thought her abilities were lacking and that the quality of music was inferior as a result. Lance asked Brian if he would intervene and try to get the elder to apologize so the keyboardist would return to her role in the praise band. That problem defined the rest of Pastor Brian's morning as he made calls to the elder and to the keyboardist. Brian was relieved when the elder took responsibility for his comments and volunteered to call the woman and apologize for his offensive comments. While the elder agreed with Brian that his comments were unwise, he expressed a need to talk about the problems regarding the quality of music at some future elders' meeting. He told Brian he still felt the music needed to be improved if "this church is ever going to reach seekers." Brian agreed to bring the matter up with the elders, but asked this elder to try to work things out in the short run. As Brian hung up the phone he felt like he had dodged a bullet that could have been far more damaging.

At noon, Brian had a lunch appointment with Pete, one of the men he was trying to recruit to lead the church's small group ministry. They were to meet at noon at a local restaurant, but the man was twenty minutes late, a delay Brian could hardly afford. The lunch took a little over an hour, with the outcome remaining uncertain. The lay leader was hesitant to take on an administrative role. He said he didn't want to get bogged down in doing details and not be able to lead a small group of his own. Brian was at least encouraged that Pete would pray about taking the position and would get back to him after the worship service on Sunday with a decision.

It was almost two o'clock by the time Brian got back to his office. He had blocked out from one o'clock to three o'clock to work on his sermon. He then planned to start his preparations for the elders' meeting that followed the Wednesday senior citizens' prayer meeting and Bible study. This was to be a major meeting dealing with the budget problem facing the church since the construction of the new addition. Cost overruns made the project more expensive than expected, so budget cuts had to be made to keep the church in the black. Brian still needed to look over the material that the chairman of the elder board had sent him and look at the financial statements from the church treasurer. Just as Brian was going to begin his sermon preparation, the phone rang. It was the chairman of the elder board. He wanted to go over plans for the meeting with Brian and asked Brian "if you had seen the material I put in your office mailbox." Brian did not tell him he hadn't had time to look them over in detail. Instead, he just said he had "seen" them. Forty minutes later, the phone meeting was over and Brian went back to his sermon preparation. But now he could only think about the meeting, so he decided to go over the material in detail. So much for preparing the sermon. It would have to wait until Thursday.

It turned out to be a very late night. There was a lot of disagreement among the elders as to how to handle the financial matters. Some were incredibly upset that the building committee had not more accurately calculated the cost of the project. Others felt that taking on even more debt was not an acceptable option. Brian tried to persuade the elders that they needed to go to the congregation and ask for a special offering to help cover the costs. Maybe people would pledge to help relieve the crisis. One rather powerful elder argued that the church simply needed to take on a larger mortgage and have faith that giving would cover the extra each month. Finally, by a split vote and against the pastor's personal wishes, the elders decided to implement an across-the-board cut of 20 percent in all discretionary budget areas. Brian went home frustrated because he knew how discouraging that decision would be to the laypeople who labored in the many programs of the church.

It was 11:38 when Brian's head finally hit the pillow. But sleep didn't come until much later. For thirty minutes he lay in bed recounting the day to his wife and sharing the tensions of the meeting. As they talked, he openly contemplated getting his résumé together to send out to another church. He was disillusioned. He had thought he would spend his time developing sermons, teaching the Word of God, and equipping lay people to do the work of the ministry. Instead, his ministry was more like the role of an executive or manager than one of shepherd-teacher.

Brian and his wife decided to stay put. After all, it isn't easy to move a family once they settle in, and anyway, another church wouldn't necessarily be any different. As a matter of survival, Brian decided to read books on management and leadership. He attended a couple of seminars to recast his idea of his role as a pastor. Eventually, over time, he took the role of the church's CEO and began to manage the church based on the concepts he had learned in his reading and research. But somehow, down inside, he felt something was compromised. He was succeeding as a church manager but failing as a godly leader.

A CASE STUDY IN PRIORITY SETTING

Once, in the earliest days of the first-century church, the leader-teachers of the Jerusalem congregation were experiencing struggles similar to those Brian Hill faced. They too were being drawn away from the priority of teaching the Word of God to the always-demanding task of managing the church. A problem had arisen in the young church, a problem of politics and prejudice. Factional interests intermingled with valid issues of human need. Though the church began as the epitome of the ideal community (Acts 4:32), it wasn't long before that community was divided. The two groups that were in disagreement were the Hebraic Jews and the Grecian Jews. Acts 6:1–7 records the account for us.

> In those days when the number of disciples was increasing, the Grecian Jews among them complained against the Hebraic Jews because their widows were being overlooked in the daily distribution of food. So the Twelve gathered all the disciples together and said, "It would not be right for us to neglect the ministry of the word of God in order to wait on tables. Brothers, choose seven men from among you who are known to be full of the Spirit and wisdom. We will turn this responsibility over to them and will give our attention to prayer and the ministry of the word."
>
> This proposal pleased the whole group. They chose Stephen, a man full of faith and of the Holy Spirit; also Philip, Procorus, Nicanor, Timon, Parmenas, and Nicolas from Antioch, a convert to Judaism. They presented these men to the apostles, who prayed and laid their hands on them.
>
> So the word of God spread. The number of disciples in Jerusalem increased rapidly, and a large number of priests became obedient to the faith.

So who were these Hebraic and Grecian Jews, and what caused the division among them? The rift between the Grecian and Hebraic Jews was essentially along cultural, linguistic, and geographic lines. The Grecian Jews, also known as Hellenistic Jews, spoke Greek and had once lived in dispersion outside of Palestine. However, when peaceful times under Roman rule allowed, they permanently resettled in Jerusalem. In a sense, they were much like the Zionist Jews who, around the turn of the twentieth century, began returning to their Palestinian homeland, or like the Orthodox Jews of today who have immigrated to Israel in our times. Likewise, these first-century, foreign-born Jews were viewed with disfavor by the native Jews; that is, the Hebraic Jews, for they possessed a different language, different values, and a different culture.

The Hebraic Jews considered themselves superior to the Hellenists. They were born in Jerusalem and worshiped in synagogues where Aramaic and Hebrew were spoken. They looked at the Grecian Jews as second-class citizens. Separating themselves from one another, the Grecians and the Hebraic Jews would have little or no communication with their brethren. This lack of communication between the groups also fostered a deep sense of bitterness on both sides.

As the church in Jerusalem grew (Acts 6:1), both Hebraic and Grecian Jews came into the church in greater and greater numbers. Unfortunately, it is not surprising that some of the prejudices between the two groups had carried over into the church. The work of Christ in the life of God's people is always a work in progress. While we are new creatures in a legal sense (2 Corinthians 5:17), we have a long way to go to become like Christ in daily experience. Long-standing and deeply held prejudice is one of those sins for which the process of transformation seems all too slow. In the Jerusalem church, the Grecian Jews experienced discrimination. Perhaps the slight was not intentional, but it was nonetheless real. Luke implies that the Grecians were a neglected minority and not well served by the church.

The specific crisis involved the care of the Grecian Jewish widows. We read that they "were being overlooked in the daily distribution of food" (Acts 6:1). Apparently, the church had organized a food distribution for the needy offering daily assistance, and the widows from the Grecian Jewish community were not being consistently cared for. This created a crisis with the potential of splitting the church.

This was no incidental problem. While genuine, the aid issue was only a surface problem. The real issue was conflict between church factions. At any rate, it is important to note how the apostles handled this important but divisive situation. It was tempting, I am sure, for them to jump in and try to take control of the conflict. Wisely, the leader-teachers understood that if they did personally manage the conflict it was likely that they would "neglect the ministry of the word of God" (6:2). Instead, they delegated the matter to others.

A proposal was made and approved by all parties. Seven people were chosen to oversee the distribution of food. The criteria for their selection were that they be men "known to be full of the Spirit and wisdom" (6:3). The plan was implemented and succeeded. It is interesting to note that all seven of the names of the new deacons were Greek. This meant that the new deacons were respected by both groups, especially by those who had lodged the complaint. What were the results? The fruit was sixfold:

- The widows were cared for.
- The church remained unified.
- Godly people were empowered to get a job done.
- Leadership was shared.
- The leader-teachers were freed to teach.
- The Word of God spread.

RECAPTURING THE PRIORITY OF TEACHING

Changes in the life of the contemporary church have created a crisis of leadership. It is not a crisis that arises from a lack of leaders so much as it is a crisis resulting from leaders who are caught on a treadmill doing good things while failing at the most basic things. The demands of a contemporary church and, in some cases, an incorrect philosophy of ministry, have repositioned the pastor into the role of church CEO and away from the biblical role as the shepherd-teacher.

What has been the cost? The sheep are not being fed. They are weak and are easy prey for the wolves that seek to devour them. Churches are growing, buildings are being built, but the people of God live in ignorance of the Word of God, and the hard-fought battle for the authority of Scripture seems to be in danger of being surrendered to other authorities. And the leaders themselves are disillusioned or, worse yet, they are deceived about their role. If you, as a contemporary leader, are to recapture the priority of teaching in your leadership ministry it will take two acts on your part. The first is a decision; the second is the recalibration of your ministry priorities around three basic activities.

Decide to Make Teaching Your Priority

The shepherding role carries the responsibility of feeding the flock. Leaders must provide spiritual food and protection for God's people through the clear proclamation of the Word of God. "Devote yourself to the public reading of Scripture, to preaching and to teaching," was Paul's exhortation to his apprentice, Timothy (1 Timothy 4:13). Clearly, priority is on the communication of the Word of God in this passage as the chief focus of the biblical leader.

Paul did not exhort Timothy to "devote yourself to the development of a mission statement, to strategic planning, to leading change, or to managing conflict." Of course, there is nothing wrong with these tasks, but they are not the most important task of the biblical leader. They are lesser matters than the matter of teaching. As most Christian leaders can attest, staying on the main task of teaching is something of a challenge when the demands of leading the church get pragmatic and sometimes political. So many other matters—needful matters—crowd teaching into the recessed corners of the leader's world.

Jim is the pastor of a small but growing church in southern Indiana, just a short distance from Louisville, Kentucky. I knew Jim as a doctoral student in the Ph.D. program I supervise at Southern Baptist Theological Seminary. Jim is a leader. He is a leader not because his church is one of the top fifty churches of its size in the Southern Baptist Convention. Jim is a leader not because of his success, status, or standing. Jim is a leader because of his walk with Christ and his teaching ministry. Through these basic and enduring leadership fundamentals, Jim is having an impact on the lives of those who hear him week after week. He is not perfect, of course, but his goals are rightly focused. Jim consistently seeks to be a faithful servant of Christ through teaching, preaching, and pastoring God's people. His church may never be a megachurch, but his leadership is every bit as effective as the pastor of the largest Baptist church south of the Mason-Dixon Line. That's because Jim's goal is to be a teacher-leader. Jim is trying to avoid being taken in by the deceptively attractive snare of the pastor-as-CEO mentality. While there is much to be learned from the corporate leaders of this world, Christian leaders must recapture and rediscover the biblical role of the leader—that of being a godly teacher of the Word of God.

You see, in the final analysis, Christian leaders lead first through the example of their lives and then through their teaching. Vision statements, strategic plans, and purpose-driven models all have their place. Nevertheless, these are not the primary means of leadership in ministry. These are secondary tools in leadership compared to the life and teaching of the leader. Once leaders forget that teaching is job number one, they diminish their eternal impact by accepting a standard only esteemed by human beings and surrendering the standard applied by God.

Recalibrate Your Heart for Teaching

So what do you have your heart set on? Do you remember the movie *A Christmas Story*? It was the story of Ralphie and his heart's desire. The film is set in the Midwest of the 1940s and follows Ralphie and the outcome of his request for a "Genuine Red Ryder Carbine Action 200-Shot Lightning Loader Range Model Air Rifle with a Shock-Proof High Adventure Combination Trail Compass and Sundial Set Right in the Stock." Ralphie makes his longing known to his mother, his teacher, and even Santa Claus at the local department store. In a "masterful work of comic silliness," the film's authority figures give Ralphie the same response: "You'll shoot your eye out." That was the warning, but he was undeterred in his heart's desire. Like Ralphie, the little boy in that movie, do you long for something with your entire heart and being?

As leaders there are a number of things that pull at our hearts. The desire to grow a ministry, the longing for recognition, and the development of our careers strive for the attention of our hearts. Then there are the many ministry needs of hurting people around us. They too call forth the better aspects of our leader's heart. It is tempting to set our hearts on these and other legitimate concerns. But if we are to lead with the greatest impact, we must recalibrate our hearts around the ministry of teaching. My proposal is simple. We need to set our hearts on the Word of God—to study it, to practice it, and to teach it to others.

Ezra is introduced to us in the seventh chapter of this small Old Testament book that bears his name. In Jewish tradition, Ezra is considered the second Moses. Moses led the people out of bondage and *gave* the people the law of the Lord. Ezra led God's people out of bondage and *preserved* God's law during a time of persecution and dispersion. Ezra was a man of God, a priest, used by God in the return of the children of Israel to Jerusalem from bondage in Babylon. Ezra was called by God to lead the people of God in rebuilding the temple and in the reestablishment of worship there in 458 BC.

One of the remarkable things about Ezra was that God blessed his leadership because of his priorities. Three times we are told, "the hand of the Lord his God was upon him." In the book of Ezra, we read this about this prophet of God.

> This Ezra went up from Babylon, and he was a scribe skilled in the law of Moses, which the Lord God of Israel had given; and the king granted him all he requested because *the hand of the Lord his God was upon him.*
>
> For on the first of the first month he began to go up from Babylon; and on the first of the fifth month he came to Jerusalem, because *the good hand of his God was upon him.*

Blessed be the Lord, the God of our fathers, who has put such a thing as this in the king's heart, to adorn the house of the Lord which is in Jerusalem, and has extended loving-kindness to me before the king and his counselors and before all the king's mighty princes. Thus I was strengthened according to *the hand of the Lord my God upon me*, and I gathered leading men from Israel to go up with me. (Ezra 7:6, 9, 27–28 NASB, italics added)

God's hand on Ezra was manifested in the amazing things that were being done through him, things only God could do. Think of it—God had moved the heart of a pagan king to allow Ezra to travel to Jerusalem to reestablish worship in the temple, and to bring back to Jerusalem the wealth of the temple that had been taken from it. Ezra was certain it was God's hand in these events. God was showing Himself in Ezra's ministry, for not only was his travel sanctioned by King Artaxerxes; it was funded as well. What no one could ever have predicted, God did! Ezra realized that God was in it, and that God had done it through him.

Wouldn't it be amazing if you could know for certain that the hand of God would be upon you in your ministry? Wouldn't it be exciting to see God do some work through you, a work that only God could do? Imagine that you, like Ezra, could say with certainty that "the hand of my Lord was upon me." But this raises an important question. What did Ezra do that caused the hand of God to be upon him? What was it that God honored in Ezra's life and ministry that led God to so bless him? Ezra spells it out for us in verses nine and ten.

For on the first of the first month he began to go up from Babylon; and on the first of the fifth month he came to Jerusalem, because the good hand of his God was upon him. For [because] Ezra had *set his heart* to study the law of the Lord and to practice it, and to teach His statutes and ordinances in Israel. (7:9–10 NASB, italics added)

Why was the hand of God on Ezra? The good hand of his God was upon him because Ezra "set his heart" on the law of the Lord, the Word of God. The word used here for "set" means "to prepare or devote oneself to something." It has the idea of "setting a course" at sea or selecting a goal or path. It means to "calibrate" or "recalibrate" an instrument. Notice three aspects to his heart commitment.

EZRA SET HIS HEART TO STUDY THE WORD OF GOD. As a student of Scripture, he had set his heart to gain thorough knowledge of God's Word. Even though he lived in a culture opposed to the God of Scripture, Ezra became known as a student of the Scriptures. Ezra understood that the Word of God is like a map for life. It lays out a course for us that orders life and guides ministry. Ezra understood that the Scriptures provide the wisdom we need for daily living and the theological foundation we need to think clearly about life's issues, ideas, and claims to truth. The Bible is our map, our guide, our norm for all matters of faith and practice. The Reformers used the phrase *Sola Scriptura*—the Scripture alone—to describe this role of the Bible. It is our measure, our light, and our standard in this present darkness. It is our one sure criterion by which we can judge truth claims and truth contributions from other sources. The Bible is not the only stream from which truth can be drawn, but it is the only pure stream against which claims to truth can be judged.

Why then, if the Bible can give such clear direction and guidance, do we fail to study it? Many Christians—I would venture to say most Christians—rarely study the Bible. The Bible has the power to enlighten us to the mind and will of God. It also has the power to enable us to follow that will. But we often fail to read it and we seldom set our hearts on studying it. Why is that? The problem, as I see it, is that the Bible does more than enlighten us to God's will and equip us to do God's will by the granting of wisdom and guidance. It also exposes sin in our lives, and that fact can drive us away from God's Word. But not Ezra. Ezra set his heart to study that sure Word of God.

EZRA SET HIS HEART TO PRACTICE THE WORD OF GOD. Ezra had determined that he would be a doer of the word, not merely a hearer. Unlike many of the Scribes and Pharisees of Jesus' time, Ezra was concerned with actually living out what he had studied in the Scriptures. Ezra understood that a study of the Word of God has a tendency to reveal the needs in our lives and the darkness in our hearts. There are times that the light of the Word shines in the corners of our lives and calls us to change. Ezra was willing to make the changes that the Word of God required.

As a young pastor of a church located in the mountains of Colorado, I found that part of my responsibilities as pastor included caring for the parsonage provided by the church. The home was a small mountain house that needed quite a bit of regular maintenance. The most recurring problem was the unreliable water system. The home was built over an old mine. Water was pumped from the mine to a holding tank located under a hatch door in the living room closet. On more than one occasion, it was my task to climb down into the cellar, a cramped dirt-floored crawl space, in order to repair the pump. Each time the breakdown occurred, I ventured into the dark crawl space with flashlight and tools in hand. But I never relished that task. Beyond the fact that the faulty pump was an annoyance, I have this major phobia when it comes to spiders, and that cellar was just the place to find those little critters.

One day when the pump broke down for what was probably the sixth time since moving in, I finally had a brilliant idea. I decided that it would be wise to install an electric light in the cellar to make my repair task a bit easier, reasoning that if I had to do this repair every few weeks, I might as well have some light to do the work by. So, taking my flashlight in hand, I shone the light around the cellar in search of an appropriate place to hang the light fixture. As I moved the beam, something caught my eye. It was a clump of spiderwebs. Something was hanging from the ceiling, almost totally encased in webs. Slowly I pushed away the webs discovering that they hid—a light bulb! Apparently my predecessor had the same idea. I pulled the string and the entire cellar was illuminated. I was unnerved to discover that spiders were all around me. Hundreds of them. Well, I did what any wise person in such situation would do: I extinguished the light, finished the pump repair, and quickly got out of that cellar.

As the light illuminated that cellar of our mountain home, exposing the webs and the spiders, so too does the light of Scripture, when studied faithfully, illumine the cellar of our lives. And too often, we simply choose to extinguish the light rather than clear the cellar. One of the functions of the Bible is that it exposes sin in our lives. In its exposing comes a clear need to change. Ezra had set his heart to practice the Word of God. That meant letting it shape his life. He was unwilling to be like the man James describes in James 1:22–25 (NASB).

> But prove yourselves doers of the word, and not merely hearers who delude themselves. For if anyone is a hearer of the word and not a doer, he is like a man who looks at his natural face in a mirror; for once he has looked at himself and gone away, he has immediately forgotten what kind of person he was. But one who looks intently at the perfect law, the law of liberty, and abides by it, not having become a forgetful hearer but an effectual doer, this man will be blessed in what he does.

Over the years, as I have seen students go into service for Christ, several have succeeded and some have failed. More often than not, failure was not due to a lack of skill, but from a lack of application of the Word of God to the student's own life. Sometimes that lack of application came as moral failure. Other times, it was simply a lack of credibility needed to minister the Word effectively. Credibility comes from living out what we study. You will never be perfect, but you must honestly and fervently strive to live that Word you study. The hand of God was upon Ezra because he set his heart to study the Word of God and to practice the Word of God. There was one more aspect to this commitment to Scripture that was foundational to his heart's desire.

EZRA SET HIS HEART TO TEACH THE WORD OF GOD. Ezra understood a significant principle related to the blessing of God—God's blessing flows out of a heart for ministry. Ezra longed to teach the Word of God to the people of God. It was that desire that was the key to God's hand being on Ezra's life. It was not enough that he studied and even practiced God's Word. The servant of God must teach it as well. Communicating the Scripture to others is part of each believer's responsibility.

Now I can imagine what you might be thinking at this juncture. You're thinking, *I don't have the gift of teaching.* While we might not be as gifted at communicating the Word as others, all of us are expected to pass along our study in some way. Not having the gift of teaching does not free us from the responsibility to teach others any more than not having the gift of hospitality frees us from being hospitable. Or not having the gift of giving, frees us from giving. Or not having the gift of faith, frees us from exercising faith. You get the point. Teaching is part of the Great Commission, and it is essential to a life blessed by God.

Not every leader will teach God's Word in a public way. Your teaching might be in a small group or one-on-one. You might do it in your home with your children or in your church with someone else's children. Wherever the teaching context, God's hand is on those who desire to communicate His Word with faithfulness. It is His primary means of leading His people.

Teaching the Word of God is a commitment God will honor in your leadership ministry. He will bless His Word. Your teaching ministry might take any number of forms. As Deuteronomy 6 mandates, you should find yourself teaching the Word in the common experiences of life. In whatever way, in whatever context, we who lead must set our hearts to teach the Word of God. Make the ministry of teaching the Word a priority whether you lead in a classroom or in discipling adolescents; whether in the pulpit or in a counseling session, keep in mind that you need to be a person of the Book. Set your heart to be one who seeks to communicate God's Word as a central part of your walk with God.

God's Word was the focus of Ezra's heart, and God blessed that commitment. His hand was on Ezra's life. A leader whose heart is given to the ministry of teaching will see results. Results not measured in the size of a budget or in the growth of the church, but results seen in the lives of people and the maturing of Christ followers. When our hearts are rightly set on diligent study of the Word, when our hearts are set on practicing the Word in our day-to-day lives, when our hearts are set on teaching that life-changing Word to others, we will see the hand of God on us, and God will do what we could never imagine—for His hand will be upon us.

Chapter Three

MORE LIKE JESUS THAN JACK:
LEARNING TO LEAD LIKE JESUS

When Jesus landed and saw a large crowd, he had compassion on them, because they were like sheep without a shepherd. So he began teaching them many things.

—Mark 6:34

TEACHING is risky business. The risk is that the lives we live will not be congruent with the words we weave. Author and educator Parker Palmer put it this way: "Teaching is always done at the dangerous intersection of personal and public life."[1] For those willing to enter that intersection, a form of leadership is in their reach—leadership more influential than any motivational speech, mission statement, or masterfully designed strategic plan.

You see, teachers have enormous influence. Long after they depart from this earth, their words and ideas continue to have a life-changing impact. Teachers leave the incomparable legacy of learning because the truths they have communicated continue to be passed on beyond their immediate students as well. Thus, teaching is an enormous responsibility because it is an extremely powerful method of leadership. In fact, when it comes to leading the people of God, it is the most powerful means of bringing genuine and lasting change.

Whether through the writings and the law of Moses, the narratives of the Historical Books, the poetry of the Psalms, the wisdom of Proverbs, the "Thus says the Lord" statements of the Prophets, the words of Jesus in the Gospels, the Acts of the Apostles, the Epistles, or the book of Revelation, the Bible is a teaching book. It is a book designed to instruct the people of God in the ways and will of God. And in the absence of its teaching, the people of God run wild. Leadership of the people of God comes from faithfully teaching the Word of God.

One of the most common verses in the Old Testament used to emphasize the need for visionary leaders is Proverbs 29:18. We hear it most often quoted in the context of church fund-raising campaigns or in books calling forth leaders. The King James Version wording reads, "Where there is no vision, the people perish." Sounds familiar, doesn't it? A call to visionary leadership, right? Wrong! This is a call to teach God's revealed Word in order to avoid the problem of God's people living godless lives. The point of this verse can be best understood by reading the entirety of the verse in contemporary English. "Where there is no revelation, the people cast off restraint; but blessed is he who keeps the law." To put it another way, where the teaching of the Word of God is absent, the people run wild!

God, in His graciousness, has blessed us with His Word and with leaders to teach it, so that we might be led to do His will. Without leaders who faithfully and accurately teach God's Word, the people of God are like sheep without a shepherd. They lack direction and care. They hunger and are endangered by the subtle and tempting heresies of the wolf-like false teachers of this world. Peter states this problem in very clear, no-nonsense words in 2 Peter 2:1–2.

> But there were also false prophets among the people, just as there will be false teachers among you. They will secretly introduce destructive heresies, even denying the sovereign Lord who bought them—bringing swift destruction on themselves. Many will follow their shameful ways and will bring the way of truth into disrepute.

Peter understood the existence of both truth and lies. Clearly, a standard of absolute, propositional truth must have been in his thinking, for he warned his readers of those who would teach "destructive heresies." How can one discern destructive heresies without an unambiguous understanding of constructive truth? Certainly, Peter would not be comfortable with the postmodern, emergent church's uncertainty about propositional truth.[2] No, he was certain that truth existed and that teaching the truth makes a vast difference in leading the people of God. Peter, like the apostle Paul, understood that "savage wolves will come in among you and will not spare the flock" (Acts 20:29). He knew that Satan's primary method of leadership is through false teaching and that God's primary method of leadership is to teach that which is true. That is why he called his readers to remain firmly established in the truth (2 Peter 1:12) and reminded them that the Scriptures were not subject to personal interpretation and were not of mere human origin (2 Peter 1:20), but are in fact, the very Word of God, inspired by the Spirit of God (2 Peter 1:21).

How did Peter come to understand that leadership of God's people flows out of teaching God's Word and allowing God's people to feed on its life-giving truth? He received his teachings from his teacher—Jesus—that's how.

THE LEADERSHIP FAILURE OF JESUS

Jesus was not a great leader! That's right! You don't have to read that statement again because you read it right the first time. A great teacher, certainly, but a great leader? Hardly. It can even be argued that, by contemporary standards, Jesus was a failure as a leader. Sure, He drew crowds of followers, but just as adeptly, He repelled people as well. Even His closest advisors, His own disciples, questioned His ability to lead. I have attended several pastors' conferences over the years, and I can tell you without question, a leader like Jesus would never be invited to be a breakout session facilitator, let alone the keynote speaker. No, He was just too ineffective as a model of leadership. Really, what did He do that made Him a great leader? I understand that we are called by good men like Kenneth Blanchard to "Lead Like Jesus."[3] Yeah, right! I doubt Jesus could even get a book published on His leadership theory. Who would read it? Yes, I know that Laurie Beth Jones has written the book *Jesus, CEO*,[4] and has done a fine job drawing on the wisdom of Jesus for today's executives, but wait—just how far should we go with following the leadership style of Jesus? What leader wants to end up crucified by those he seeks to lead?

Jack Welch, now there is a leader to follow! Pastors would do well to emulate his style and practice of leadership. Jack, as his followers know him, was the chairman and CEO of General Electric. During his role as chief executive, GE increased its market value by more than $400 billion over just two decades. Now that is *success*. "The two greatest corporate leaders of this century are Alfred Sloan of General Motors and Jack Welch of GE," says Noel Tichy, author of *The Cycle of Leadership*. "And Welch would be the greater of the two because he set a new, contemporary paradigm for the corporation that is the model for the 21st century."[5] Now that is *status*. Welch, when CEO, sat atop a business empire with $304 billion in assets, $89.3 billion in sales, and 276,000 employees scattered in more than a hundred countries around the globe. Welch has reshaped the company through more than six hundred acquisitions and led a forceful push abroad into newly emerging markets.[6] Now that is *standing*. How can Jesus compete with that kind of record as a leader?

Then again, maybe the problem in evaluating Jesus' leadership skill is the standard itself. The common standard of great leadership is one most often drawn from the world of business, sports, the military, and politics. From that perspective, the issues of *success*, *status*, and *standing* are the most typical measures of leadership prowess. Jesus lacked all three.

Jesus Enjoyed Little and Short-Lived Success

When Jesus did miracles, most people came for the show, not to actually follow His leadership. True, a few did follow, but many more were simply in awe of His abilities. As a result, for a brief time His band of followers grew, but in the end, when confronted with the realities of being His disciple, not one stood by Him as their leader. He had the crowds but failed to keep them. He had a close band of dedicated under-studies, but when He needed their allegiances, they denied they even knew Him. Even His most promising apprentice, Peter, went to great lengths to avoid association with Jesus when it meant personal sacri-fice. No great organization, no great group of followers—so much for success.

Jesus Did Little to Gain and Retain Status

Respected as a rabbi by many, Jesus had the crowds singing His praises in the streets. However, where it really counted, Jesus failed to gain status with the power people of His day. If He were a great leader by today's standards, Jesus would have "networked" far more effec-tively with the likes of Pontius Pilate and Herod Antipas. Had He done so, He would have had their backing when He really needed it . . . that is, if He were a great leader by contemporary standards. Even with the masses, Jesus' status slipped significantly during that last week of His life. You see, Judas understood that Jesus lacked the ability He needed to manage His image. The result was that a promising role as king and leader was lost. Jesus could have occupied a significant leadership in-fluence if He had just played His cards right.

Jesus Lacked Social or Political Standing

Jesus never held any position of power. He never made it to the position of king or even high priest. He lacked entrepreneurialism and never became a prominent CEO. He was never a manager or senior executive, and He certainly never rose to be a leader of an insurgent force against the occupying Romans. He was not even a religious leadership opportunist. He never led a large church or synagogue and had no résumé of ladder-climbing positions. No, the fact is that He never sought nor occupied a position of authority. Once, He was known to have renounced the notion of "lord[ing] it over" others (Matthew 20:25–26) and preferred to make Himself a servant. He even encouraged His followers to practice His servant role by modeling it (John 13:14). Totally out of the character of the leader, Jesus washed His disciples' feet—an act of a mere slave, not a chief executive. What kind of standing is that? No standing, no status, and no success! Not much of a leader by contemporary standards, but then, that depends on whether you accept that standard, doesn't it?

An Alternative Standard of Leadership

We have been hoodwinked. We have come to accept a standard for leadership that actually robs the church of great leaders. The standing-status-success standard is not a biblical standard; it is the world's standard. Pastors are not to be CEOs, and our best models are not corporate executives, coaches, generals, and presidents. Far from it. While much can be learned about leadership from corporate CEOs, team coaches, military generals, and politicians, the biblical leader is, first and foremost, a skilled and godly shepherd-teacher. Frankly, I have nothing against Jack Welch, but I am convinced that the Christian leader—whether pastor, staff member, college or seminary president, church elder or academic dean, Sunday school teacher, club leader, and so on—is to be far more like Jesus than Jack when it comes to leadership.

Jesus used a figure of speech, a metaphor, to describe Himself. In John 10:1–18, Jesus tells us that He is the Good Shepherd. Here, a different standard of leadership is established by which we should evaluate Jesus as leader.

"I tell you the truth, the man who does not enter the sheep pen by the gate, but climbs in by some other way, is a thief and a robber. The man who enters by the gate is the shepherd of his sheep. The watchman opens the gate for him, and the sheep listen to his voice. He calls his own sheep by name and leads them out. When he has brought out all his own, he goes on ahead of them, and his sheep follow him because they know his voice. But they will never follow a stranger; in fact, they will run away from him because they do not recognize a stranger's voice." Jesus used this figure of speech, but they did not understand what he was telling them.

Therefore Jesus said again, "I tell you the truth, I am the gate for the sheep. All who ever came before me were thieves and robbers, but the sheep did not listen to them. I am the gate; whoever enters through me will be saved. He will come in and go out, and find pasture. The thief comes only to steal and kill and destroy; I have come that they may have life, and have it to the full.

"I am the good shepherd. The good shepherd lays down his life for the sheep. The hired hand is not the shepherd who owns the sheep. So when he sees the wolf coming, he abandons the sheep and runs away. Then the wolf attacks the flock and scatters it. The man runs away because he is a hired hand and cares nothing for the sheep.

"I am the good shepherd; I know my sheep and my sheep know me—just as the Father knows me and I know the Father—and I lay down my life for the sheep. I have other sheep that are not of this sheep pen. I must bring them also. They too will listen to my voice, and there shall be one flock and one shepherd. The reason my Father loves me is that I lay down my life—only to take it up again. No one takes it from me, but I lay it down of my own accord. I have authority to lay it down and authority to take it up again. This command I received from my Father." (John 10:1–18)

As the Good Shepherd, Jesus tells us several things about how He leads His followers. First, *He leads His followers through the power of personal relationship.* Speaking of the Judean shepherds, Jesus says, " . . . the sheep listen to his voice. He calls his own sheep by name and leads them out. When he has brought out all his own, he goes on ahead of them, and his sheep follow him because they know his voice" (vv. 3–4). Like those shepherds of the first century, Jesus tells us that, "I know my sheep and my sheep know me" (v. 14). Later in this passage, in verse 27 Jesus states that, "My sheep listen to my voice; I know them, and they follow me."

A second characteristic of Jesus leadership is that *He leads His followers by the act of sacrificial care*. He says that, "I am the good shepherd. The good shepherd lays down his life for the sheep" (v. 11). Again, He says, "I am the good shepherd; I know my sheep and my sheep know me—just as the Father knows me and I know the Father—and I lay down my life for the sheep" (vv. 14–15).

Third, *He leads His followers by feeding them*. Through Him, His sheep are able to find pasture. "I am the gate; whoever enters through me will be saved. He will come in and go out, and find pasture. The thief comes only to steal and kill and destroy; I have come that they may have life, and have it to the full" (vv. 9–10). The pastures to which Jesus leads His sheep are secure. His sheep can "come in and go out, and find pasture." His pastures are safe places to be where His sheep are comfortable and at ease because He is the secure and powerful gate through which that access occurs. As shepherd, Jesus feeds His sheep in pastures abundant with food. In Christ alone can we find the food that completely satisfies. He is the Bread of Life.

Here then is an alternative standard of leadership effectiveness from the standing-status-success model offered by the world. It is a standard that describes leadership in terms of personal relationship, sacrificial care, and secure and abundant provision.

JESUS CAME TEACHING

The people sought a king, someone to sit on the throne of David. Their Messiah was to come to this earth to conquer and reign. That was the expectation that even His disciples demanded of Jesus. He was to be their leader. He was to establish His kingdom and then bring the long-expected justice that the people of God so desperately desired. He was to be the king of the hill, the leader of the parade. He was to call on His angels to do His bidding and defeat His enemies with awesome force and power. However, that was not the Jesus who showed up on this planet two thousand years ago.

But Jesus came teaching. His method of leadership was to draw disciples or students around Him and then teach them. He taught using parables and metaphors. He taught with proverbs and questions. He taught using objects and demonstrations. He taught formally in the synagogues and informally in the marketplace, by a well, at a lake, on a hillside. The most common designation for Jesus was *rabbi*—teacher. Clearly, Jesus did not come as leader of an enterprise but as the teacher of the words that bring life. It was His teaching and His sacrifice that marked His leadership.

It was probably one of the heaviest periods of ministry Jesus had experienced up to this juncture and, it is clear from the Scriptures, Jesus was feeling the strain of it all. At the beginning of Mark 6 we discover that Jesus makes a trip to His hometown where He speaks in the synagogue. There His teaching was critiqued and rejected because of a lack of faith on the part of those who knew Him best (Mark 6:1–5). Rather than stay near home where responsiveness was low, Jesus launched out on an itinerant ministry, speaking from village to village (6:6–7). The pace must have been grueling. Soon after, in an effort to multiply His effectiveness and develop His disciples, He implemented a plan to send His disciples out to preach, teach, and heal the sick (6:8–13). While His disciples were busy sharing the message of repentance, Jesus received the sad news of the beheading of John the Baptist by King Herod (6:14–29). In the midst of this tragic time of personal loss, His disciples returned to report on their ministry assignments. Gathering the apostles around Him in a "staff meeting" of sorts, His team debriefed Jesus on the effectiveness of their teaching ministries. But the crowds who wanted to be with Jesus interrupted the meeting constantly. The people were coming and going on a nonstop basis, so much so that Jesus found Himself unable to even eat a meal in private. Finally, in an attempt to retreat with His disciples Jesus makes this statement in Mark 6:31–32.

> "Come with me by yourselves to a quiet place and get some rest."
> So they went away by themselves in a boat to a solitary place.

But they were unable to break away from the crowds. The people saw Him and His disciples get into a boat, so they raced ahead of Him on foot and got to the place He was heading before He landed (6:32–33). Though He may have been close to exhaustion, Jesus was moved with compassion toward these devoted followers. In verse 34 we read these remarkable words.

> When Jesus landed and saw a large crowd, he had compassion on them, because they were like sheep without a shepherd. So he began teaching them many things.

Notice what Jesus' response was to these hungry people. Seeing them as sheep without a shepherd; that is, as needy, leaderless followers, He responds by teaching them many things. Jesus' first leadership response to these shepherdless persons was a teaching response. He follows this by feeding them physically as well, but it is not their physical need that struck His heart first, but their need to know the truth that could set them free. Jesus led by teaching, and He calls those who lead His sheep to do the same.

Feed My Sheep: The Call to Biblical Leadership

Three times Peter denied Jesus. Three times, he was asked if he was with Jesus, and every single time swore he did not know the man that he had said he would unswervingly follow. It was just as

Jesus predicted. "I tell you the truth," Jesus answered, "this very night, before the rooster crows, you will disown me three times" (Matthew 26:34). Peter was defeated—a broken servant, believing he was no longer fit for ministry in the kingdom. In the pit of despair, Peter returned to the sea that he knew so well as a fisherman. With his hands upon the nets, Peter struggled to deal with his denial of Jesus. It was there, on the beach, that Jesus came to Peter to restore him to service in the kingdom of God. Jesus pulled Peter from the wreckage of his threefold denial by asking him a question and by giving him a task.

> Jesus said to Simon Peter, "Simon son of John, do you truly love me more than these?"
>
> "Yes, Lord," he said, "you know that I love you."
>
> Jesus said, "Feed my lambs."
>
> Again Jesus said, "Simon son of John, do you truly love me?"
>
> He answered, "Yes, Lord, you know that I love you."
>
> Jesus said, "Take care of my sheep."
>
> The third time he said to him, "Simon son of John, do you love me?"
>
> Peter was hurt because Jesus asked him the third time, "Do you love me?" He said, "Lord, you know all things; you know that I love you."
>
> Jesus said, "Feed my sheep." (John 21:15–17)

Three times, Jesus' question to Peter was simply this—Peter, do you love Me? Peter's reply all three times was a clear yes. At each response, Jesus called Peter to a task—to feed and care for His sheep. As Jesus restores Peter back into kingdom service, we see something of the kind of person God uses in ministry and the method by which He makes use of them. God uses those who are repentant. Peter had sinned grossly. Of all things, he had abandoned and disavowed Jesus publicly. But in recognition of his sin we are told that Peter wept bitterly (Luke 22:62). Jesus responded to the repentant heart of His servant and welcomed him back to kingdom ministry. This demonstration of care on the part of Jesus holds out great hope to all kinds of failed followers.

Jesus is pleased to offer forgiveness to the repentant, but with forgiveness comes a call to serve. In the case of this leader, and in the case of all who seek to lead the people of God, it is a call to teach. The essence of biblical leadership is summed up in the command of Jesus to Peter, "Feed my sheep."

Shepherding God's Flock

Shepherds do more than feed the sheep. Of course, feeding is the priority, but other actions are needed if the sheep are to be fed. Jesus also told Peter to "take care of my sheep." That is a stewardship command. Stewards care for the belongings of another. A steward is an extension of the owner and is to have the same level of care as the owner would for those belongings. In a real sense, biblical shepherds—that is, the pastor-teachers of Ephesians 4:11—are stewards of the flock of God. As such, biblical leaders have a sacred trust for which they will give an account. Peter later exhorted elders to "Be shepherds of God's flock that is under your care" (1 Peter 5:2). As overseers, elders are to "keep watch over [the church] as men who must give an account" (Hebrews 13:17). To the elders of the church at Ephesus, Paul urged accountability as shepherds of the church of God with these words.

> Keep watch over yourselves and all the flock of which the Holy Spirit has made you overseers. Be shepherds of the church of God, which he bought with his own blood. I know that after I leave, savage wolves will come in among you and will not spare the flock. Even from your own number men will arise and distort the truth in order to draw away disciples after them. So be on your guard! (Acts 20:28–31)

Simple observations of this passage yield some important shepherding principles. First, biblical leaders must genuinely care for the people under their leadership oversight. Second, biblical leaders must be prepared for "savage wolves" to arise in their own midst, bent on distorting the truth and drawing the sheep away. And third, biblical leaders must be on their guard. Leaders cannot be lulled into a sense of complacency. They must be aware that they are engaged in a battle for the truth. It is with false teaching that the sheep are taken captive; thus, the Enemy is keenly aware that the struggle is, in fact, a matter of teaching the truth versus teaching error.

Leadership has been defined without reference to teaching, and as a result has been stripped of its central biblical function. Pastoral care, though encompassing more than teaching only, is *predominately* a matter of teaching. It is a leadership role involving the shepherding of the hearts and minds of followers. Unfortunately, for many churches and their leaders, the shepherding role has been separated from the teaching function of that role. Leadership has been redefined as visioncasting, executive leadership, and influence. Those roles are part of the definition of biblical leadership, but they are far less significant components than is the role of teacher. One author puts it this way:

> The fact is . . . that too many leaders are more enthusiastic about the activities of the church, the operation of its machinery, the size of its membership, the amount of its budgets, the cultural life and social problems of society, the passage of laws by legislative bodies, the promotion of human improvement programs—all of which are good and necessary—than about the gospel and the transforming power of God. To deal with the visible and the tangible is much easier and, for the time being, more interesting, perhaps more rewarding, than to deal with the invisible and the intangible.[7]

Jim Means puts it best when he writes, "Spiritual servant-leaders must realize that the central tasks that define their roles have to do with study, prayer, modeling, discipling, preaching, teaching and equipping the saints for ministry."[8]

TEACHING THE TRUTH: THE ESSENTIAL POWER OF BIBLICAL LEADERSHIP

J. Robert Clinton, author and professor of leadership, has defined a biblical leader as one who influences a specific group of people to move in a God-given *direction.*[9] God uses many different kinds of leaders to bring about the movement He desires. Some leaders influence by *positional power*, the power of their office or position. Some influence by *personal power*, the power of their example or persona. Still others lead by the power of their teaching—*persuasive power*. Let's briefly consider all three sources of leadership power in ministry.

Positional Power

Sometimes God moves His people through the commanding leadership of an office holder. Joseph (Genesis 41:41–45; 45:9), Moses (Exodus 3:10–12), and the kings of the Old Testament (1 Samuel 8:4–5), including Saul and David, are examples of positional power. In the New Testament, the apostles (2 Corinthians 12:11–12) and elders (1 Timothy 3:1–7; Titus 1:5–9) had positional power in the church. God established authorities and called His people to obey them within the bounds of biblical morality. The writer of Hebrews is abundantly clear on this when he instructs his readers to "Obey your leaders and submit to their authority. They keep watch over you as men who must give an account. Obey them so that their work will be a joy, not a burden, for that would be of no advantage to you" (Hebrews 13:17). God does establish offices in the church and appoints leaders to those offices. Those leaders have divinely granted positional power. But God also calls for a consistency between the character and lifestyle of those leaders and the office they hold. That is why the qualifications for the office of elder or deacon are predominately about matters of character and spirituality (1 Timothy 3:1–13; Titus 1:5–9).

Influenced by postmodern assumptions and the writings of leadership authors such as Peter Senge, who wrote *The Fifth Discipline*, some claim that such positional power is out of date and that it has been replaced with the power of relationships. Drawing on trends in business management, Donald Hughes writes, "Heroic leaders are out. The new focus is on creating a climate where employees are provided with a goal, then are allowed to organize themselves to meet the goal."[10] Hughes argues that, due to the influence of John D. Rockefeller Jr., a devout Baptist, churches have become "little corporations" and pastors have become unbiblical "hero" pastors. He may well be right, but while positional power is helpful to the leader, it is not required. That is because a greater power can be found in the influence of one's life, character, and relationships.

Personal Power

Personal power is not based on the office one holds but rather on the impact of one's life. Personal power is the power of relationships. Though holding no earthly office, Jesus had the ability to draw followers, influence thinking, and make change. It seems Paul also had personal leadership power. The use of personal power can be clearly seen in Paul's communication with Philemon. Having led Philemon to faith in Christ and having developed a deep personal relationship, Paul called upon that relationship to motivate Philemon to accept a runaway slave by the name of Onesimus as a Christian brother (Philemon 8–16). Through the power of a relationship, Paul exercised leadership; that is, he moved a specific group of people in a God-given direction.

Exercised together, with a godly character evident in the life of a leader, positional and personal power can be an enormous force for ministry leadership. Those qualities can grow a church and move a congregation forward. But there is a third type of leadership power needed. It is the power of persuasive ideas. Personal power persuades as well, but without substantial content it does not produce the intrinsic motivation and lasting change that alters a person's worldview. It is a change of mind along with the heart that brings about that kind of impact.

Persuasive Power

We need to be clear here. By persuasive power we are not talking about muscle or the manipulation of people through ingenious arguments or flowery speech. We are referring to the power of truth, the power of ideas, and in its most biblical sense, the power of the Word of God. Keep in mind as well that I am not suggesting that this is an either / or proposition. My point is not that positional power and personal power are wrong or inappropriate and that persuasive power is the only influence option for the biblical leader. The fact is, each of these types of power can be used in a godly manner and each can be corrupted by the sin nature. Our point is this: While positional and personal power are helpful and even mission-critical for leading the people of God, it is the persuasive power of biblical teaching that is absolutely indispensable. Persuasive power at its best occurs when followers are persuaded to follow by the authority of Scripture. In combination with the personal power of a godly character and a caring relationship with the follower, the persuasive power of teaching is the most potent of leadership forces. Leaders who exercise this kind of leadership power do so not by the authority of their own words but by the authority of God's Word.

Imagine balancing your checkbook using Roman numerals. Although a common part of our lives, the concept of base ten numbers is actually a fairly recent advancement. The use of Hindu-Arabic numbers is considered by some to be the most significant advancement in Western history. Robert T. Kiyosaki and Sharon L. Lechter point out the power of this one idea in their book *The Rich Dad's Guide to Investing*, in which they write:

> One of the most important technological changes in the history of the Western World took place during the Crusades, when Christian soldiers came across the Hindu-Arabic system of numbers. The Hindu-Arabic system of numbers, so named because the Arabs found the

numbering system during their invasion of India, replaced what we call Roman numerals. Few people appreciate the difference this new system of numbers has made upon our lives. The Hindu-Arabic system of numbers allowed people to sail farther out to sea with greater accuracy; architecture could be more ambitious; time keeping could [be] more accurate; the human mind sharpened; and people thought more accurately, abstractly, and critically.[11]

This one idea has dramatically impacted life on this planet. Through the use of ten symbols in various combinations, numbers can be formed to measure distances that stretch to the farthest galaxies or to calculate the weight of the smallest atomic particle. Opening the worlds of science, mathematics, engineering, and finance, base ten numbers have enabled colossal growth in human understanding and technological achievement.

Here is just one example that proves ideas have power to change the world. Ideas can bring lasting modifications to the very foundation on which a community, and even a culture, is built. What is more, ideas can change the life of an individual by changing their fundamental worldview. Now, here is the most remarkable thing of all—from a leadership perspective, teachers command the power of those ideas. They do so by enabling learners to grasp great thoughts and their implications of those thoughts for life. Teachers can change people by freeing learners to understand their world and, as a result, to change the circumstances in which they live. Jesus said, "You will know the truth, and the truth will set you free" (John 8:32). Read in context, Jesus was referring directly to Himself as "the way, and the truth and the life" (John 14:6), but the principle is universally true. Truth has the power to free. That is why those who seek to hold others in bondage, whether dictator, slaveholder, or political elitist, must regulate the free flow of truth through the use of propaganda, lies, ignorance, and illiteracy. That is also why Satan uses lies to place people into spiritual bondage and is, himself, the Father of Lies. Lies bind, truth frees!

Teachers lead when they teach in such a way as to free learners by the power of the truth. Likewise, leaders lead most powerfully when they tell and teach the truth. The greatest of leaders are more like Jesus than Jack. Their leadership is seen in their ability to free people by teaching the truth of the Word of God, not in their ability to grow an enterprise. While standing, status, and success are to be respected, they are not the standard by which the leaders of God's people are ultimately judged. Whether leading a megachurch or a more modest work, biblical leaders are judged by their faithfulness to their teaching call. It is encouraging to note that the pastor of the smallest church can be equally, or even more, effective as the pastor of the largest church, for the leader's call is not to build the church, but to equip the saints. That is done as leaders "speak the truth in love" (Ephesians 4:11–16) and thus, teach as Jesus taught and lead as Jesus led. You see, if we are to lead like Jesus, we must learn to teach like Jesus.

Chapter Four

LEADERSHIP BY THE BOOK:
THE COMMITMENT OF THE LEADER-TEACHER

The grass withers and the flowers fall, but the word of our God stands forever.

—Isaiah 40:8

But as for you, continue in what you have learned and have become convinced of, because you know those from whom you learned it, and how from infancy you have known the holy Scriptures, which are able to make you wise for salvation through faith in Christ Jesus. All Scripture is God-breathed and is useful for teaching, rebuking, correcting and training in righteousness, so that the man of God may be thoroughly equipped for every good work.

—2 Timothy 3:14–17

WHEN I was a student at Moody Bible Institute in the mid-seventies, my wife, Marlene, and I traveled each weekend to a church in Pontiac, Illinois, where I served as a youth pastor The hundred-mile drive was typically a pretty routine experience, with the exception of one particular Friday evening. As we traveled south on Interstate 55, a major snowstorm swept across the center of the state. It brought whiteout conditions and a disorienting feeling that was frightening. We could not see much beyond our headlights. We feared pulling over, concerned that we might be rear-ended by another motorist who could not see us stopped in front of him. We also feared going forward with no sense of whether we were on the road or heading off into the median or some embankment. With little else to go by, we simply followed the lights of a truck in front of us. He was following the truck in front of him, and so on. With the reference point of a truck's lights, we were able to continue our journey and arrive safely.

Leadership is especially challenging in the twenty-first century. In many ways, leaders today are traveling through conditions like those we experienced that winter evening. Leadership is tricky because of the cultural, philosophical, theological, and moral malaise in which we live. The new tolerance of pluralism has produced whiteout conditions on the leadership highway. Lost are the clear highway lane markers that leaders have always depended on to keep them centered and on the road. Without those boundary lines, leaders ride perilously close to the ditches that line the sides of the highway. They move forward at times just hoping they are heading the right direction. Often, leaders find themselves simply following someone else, assuming that person knows where to go. All the while, they are keenly aware that they are responsible for a line of people following close behind, people dependent on them. Without some external objective reference by which to steer, leaders can become disoriented and uncertain.

Leadership has never been easy. If it were, leaders would be in abundance. No, leadership has always been a challenge, and great leaders have been few in number. That is because leadership demands discernment, and discernment demands a knowledge of good and evil, right and wrong, truth and error, and that which is wise and/or or unwise. Discernment is the ability to choose the best among highly attractive alternatives. Great leaders know that some paths, though eye-catching at the beginning, turn out to be dead ends—or even worse, a tragic misdirection leading to unexpected consequences.

A FOUNDATIONAL COMMITMENT

It hardly seems like it should be necessary to make this statement but here goes: *Biblical leadership begins with a commitment to biblical authority.* If researchers like George Barna are correct, it no longer can be assumed that Christians understand that principle.[1] Many are no longer sure that, in this pluralistic world in which various viewpoints exist, it is desirable to hold to the exclusive claims of an authoritative, inerrant Bible as the starting point for understanding much of anything, let alone leadership. They fear that a belief in biblical authority, including the doctrines derived from that belief, spawns authoritarian leaders.

They also fear that an emphasis on a clear and established biblical orthodoxy conveys social intolerance and exclusivity. Richard Robert Osmer, a neo-orthodox, mainline Protestant author, expresses these concerns in his book *A Teachable Spirit: Recovering the Teaching Office of the Church.* He writes,

> The pretense of an unmediated orthodoxy severely limits conservative Protestantism's capacity to be self-critical and to take seriously the insight of other perspectives.[2]

Conservatives are originalists when it comes to understanding the Bible. We believe we can, through the use of careful methods of research, understand the intent and meaning of writers of the Bible. We believe that the very words of Scripture are important to understanding that intent and meaning. We believe that the Bible is the Word of God and is authoritative over all of life and practice. Similar to constitutional originalists in the arena of law, biblical originalists reject the idea that all interpretations are equally valid. Biblical originalists believe that we can teach with authority if we teach only and always the original intent and meaning of the biblical text.

Osmer disagrees. After stating that the teachings offered by such

Bible teachers, "are not timeless, nor are they derived directly from Scripture," Osmer then warns that,

> A second major weakness of contemporary conservative Protestantism is its tendency toward authoritarianism. While this characteristic is not universally present, a defensive, reactive relationship to the surrounding world and an attempt to serve as the guardian of "true" Christianity have consistently led this cultural tradition toward theological and social authoritarianism.[3]

He concludes that as mainline churches find themselves in numerical decline due to liberal theology, they should avoid turning to the authority of conservative Protestants (that being an inerrant, authoritative Bible). His alternative authority is the authority of "individual conscience and communal authority" of the church.[4]

What is of concern is not the fact that a neo-orthodox writer embraces "individual conscience and communal authority." That is to be expected. What is troubling is that so many evangelicals now comfortably agree with him.[5] These emerging leaders hold that knowledge cannot ever be purely objective and that all interpretations of the Scriptures are subjective, cultural, and personal.[6] They contend that all truth is "contextual" and, therefore, cannot be considered universal or propositional.[7] They conclude that truth is, at best, communal or tribal.[8]

In reality, what these emergent leaders propose regarding the matter of biblical authority is not new; it is simply a form of reemergent neo-orthodoxy—retitled and rereleased as the emerging church movement. It is a belief that the Bible becomes the Word of God for each individual when they have a spiritual encounter with God through its message. That encounter is entirely subjective and individual in nature (existential) and not subject to critique or judgment. The best we can do according to this point of view, is to discuss our encounters and see if any common themes emerge (communal truth) that we can agree to live by.

Despite claims to the contrary by leaders of the emergent church movement, biblical leadership must begin with an unequivocal belief in the objective truth of God's Word and its authority over both belief and practice. As Jesus prayed for His disciples, "Sanctify them by the truth; your word is truth" (John 17:17).

Jesus taught that absolute truth is knowable. He also taught that truth is found in the Word of God. Biblical leaders must take heed to Jesus' prayer. Jesus believed that the sanctification of His followers would be the result of the truth of the Word of God. Truth is not a social construct. An individual, a culture, or even a community of believers, does not create it. Nor is it relative as some claim. The God of truth, through revelation, both natural and special, communicates it to us, His creatures. He does this in diverse ways (Hebrews 1:1–3), including the use of language and propositions. Over seventy-five times Jesus proclaimed, "I tell you the truth," with a certain knowledge that truth does in fact exist.

Richard Cizik is vice president for governmental affairs for the National Association of Evangelicals. He was interviewed by the PBS show *Frontline* as part of their look at evangelicals entitled *The Jesus Factor*. Cizik hit the nail on the head when he identified the single most significant distinctive between evangelical Christians and mainline Protestants (and even the emergent church, in my estimation). When asked to define an evangelical, he said,

> I think that George Gallup's definition is probably pretty good. He says that evangelicals are those who, first of all, believe the Bible is authoritative. It's infallible. This is a theological distinction that separates evangelicals from, say, mainline Protestantism, which generally veers from that kind of designation of the Bible as the authoritative Word of God.
>
> I think there's one way to understand the evangelical view of the Bible. It is viewed as the objective, authoritative Word of God, as opposed to the mainline Protestant view called neo-orthodoxy that

holds, you see, that the Bible becomes the Word of God in a kind of existential encounter with it.

So that's the distinction. It doesn't just become the Word of God when you have an experience with God or an experience with the Word. It is objectively, authoritatively the Word of God. That's what distinguishes evangelicals from, say, mainline Protestants.[9]

This foundational commitment to the authority of Scripture marks the evangelical. It must also be the distinguishing characteristic of the biblical leader. Biblical leaders are committed to biblical authority and to the absolutes of Scripture.

I would encourage you to be wise and exercise caution here as you read materials on Christian leadership. Not all who actually say they are committed to biblical authority mean it in the classical evangelical sense as Cizik described it. There are a growing number of writers, published by well-known Christian publishers, who embrace reemergent neo-orthodoxy in their approach to the Scriptures while claiming to be evangelical.[10] There is a problem of what Millard Erikson calls "category slide" occurring in the literature, preaching, and teaching of those who would identify themselves as evangelical. Erickson describes this slide in language as follows.

A person who once was considered neo-orthodox may now be termed evangelical, and someone who formerly was clearly identified as evangelical may now be branded a fundamentalist, without the actual views of the persons involved having changed in any significant way.[11]

AVOIDING THE DITCHES

Imagine for a moment a road before you. You are in the lane called "biblical worldview." The oncoming lane can be thought of as "contemporary culture." Although not always the case, it is generally true that the "contemporary culture" lane heads in the opposing direction from the "biblical worldview" lane.

Two ditches line this road of biblical leadership, threatening your effectiveness. My encouragement is that you avoid them both with great care. The first is the ditch of *cultural accommodation*—that is, an extreme and excessive attempt at cultural relevancy. To get there you will need to swerve left of center.

The second is the ditch of *cultural isolation*—that is, a total disconnected cultural irrelevancy. You get there by making a hard turn to the right. It is difficult to say which is most dangerous. The ditch to your left requires you to cross traffic and risk a head-on collision with the postmodern philosophy of contemporary culture. The second ditch, the one on your right, is closer, but it can be just as deadly. It looks safe because you don't have to cross into the world's oncoming traffic to get there, but once you enter it, you will come to a screeching halt, mired in the mud of legalism, empty activity, and sometimes dead orthodoxy.

The Ditch of Cultural Accommodation

The first ditch you must avoid as a biblical leader is the ditch of *cultural accommodation.* By that, I do not mean that you do not seek to be relevant in our culture, but you cannot make relevancy the primary goal of leadership. If you do, you will find yourself not just seeking to relate to and understand the times, but controlled by and fully immersed in the philosophy of the times as well. Rather than be "in the world but not of it" as Jesus commanded, the world will simply be in you and your leadership will become indistinguishable from leadership practiced in the culture. Such is the case in the current attempts to embrace postmodernism by some evangelical leaders.

The Rise of Postmodernism: Truth as Fable

Postmodernism has permeated all aspects of our culture. It dominates academic disciplines, literature, the media, popular culture, and is rapidly finding its place in the church. But what exactly is post-modernism?

POSTMODERNISM IS A PROTEST RESPONSE TO MODERNISM. To understand postmodernism, one must begin with a very broad understanding of the history of Western civilization. We can divide Western history roughly into three eras: premodern, modern, and postmodern. The premodern era began in the fourth century, when Christianity became the official religion of the Roman Empire. Supernaturalism was generally a given. This period was characterized by not only belief in God, but the belief that God was at the center of truth, especially as dictated by the Roman Catholic Church. With the dawning of the Renaissance, beginning in the fourteenth century, a shift toward humanism was taking place, but it was a humanism that acknowledged God and celebrated mankind as His highest creation.

By the middle of the seventeenth century, another philosophical turn was occurring. God still existed, but He had set the world to operate on its own—not in chaos, but within the order of natural laws. The logical progression of this "enlightened" way of thinking was that man could find a basis for meaning without help from God, but through his own reason and logic.

A representative Enlightenment philosopher was Immanuel Kant (1724–1804), who began to question the long-held dogmas of the church. In an effort to free human beings from superstition, philosophers of the Enlightenment emphasized the power of rational thinking. This enlightened thinking presupposed the power of human reason to discover truth. No longer was the church the guardian of the truth.

The Enlightenment ended with the French Revolution. All the logic and reason of this age could not hold back the worst in mankind, as the ideals behind the revolution degenerated into a bloodbath.

Because reason and philosophy hadn't been able to uphold truth, it was now science that was to determine what was absolute truth, bringing in the modern era. Truth was achieved through logic and the use of the scientific method. The results were breathtaking, including the

Industrial Revolution, massive technological advancement, and gains in every area of human knowledge. So certain were the modernists that science would solve all problems that utopian promises abounded. Modernism promised an end of all war, human suffering, and societal problems through the secularization of societies where empirical truth, not mere speculation, was to determine the human future.

Sometime between World War I and the fall of the Berlin Wall, modernism began to lose its power over the culture. What was lost in the rise of modernism was the place of the supernatural. Knowledge became sterile and cold, as science ruled. Certainly, science and technology have never been more influential in daily living than they are now, but it became obvious that science did not hold the answers to the deepest questions of human existence. Science could not eliminate war, human suffering, acts of evil, or the existence of poverty and hunger. Worse yet, science stripped its followers of meaning in life as they moved to embrace its naturalistic, positivistic, and deterministic premises. So the stage was set. Move over modernism as postmodernism, in reaction, arrived as the response to these disappointments.

Postmodernism is a reaction to the failures of modernism. Disillusioned by the failure to achieve the optimistic goals of modernism, postmoderns have turned to a far more pessimistic, cynical outlook. Postmoderns have come to believe that there is no overarching truth that unifies and no ultimate story that explains our existence or this world. Postmoderns cannot accept the premodern concept that truth is found in revelation, for it is seen as too simplistic and backward. At the same time, they reject the modernistic belief that truth can be found in the use of the scientific method, for it is empty and hard. What is left is resignation. Postmoderns resign themselves to the belief that nothing can actually be known for certain, that absolute truth is a fable, and that everyone's interpretation of truth so colors their conclusions that no truth claims hold any more authority than any other claims.[12] So then, postmodernism rests on these three basic tenets regarding truth.

TRUTH IS CONSTRUCTED. Postmodern philosophy rejects the notion of self-evident or absolute truth. Rather, truth is created or "construct-ed" by the individual or the community. Because truth is a human con-struct, it is subjective and not objective. One postmodern Christian author, Donald Miller, puts it this way.

> My most recent faith struggle is not one of intellect. I don't really do that anymore. Sooner or later you just figure that there are some guys who don't believe in God and they can prove He doesn't exist, and some other guys who do believe in God and they can prove He does ex-ist, and the arguments stopped being about God a long time ago and now it's about who is smarter, and honestly I don't care. I don't believe I will ever walk away from God for intellectual reasons. Who knows anything anyway? If I walk away from Him, and please pray that I never do, I will walk away for social reasons, identity reasons, deep emotional reasons, the same reasons that any of us do anything.[13]

Who knows anything anyway? That is the heart of the postmodern understanding of truth and those who do believe they know something are simply arrogant, ignorant, or trying to pull off an authoritarian power play.

TRUTH IS RELATIVE. If truth cannot be known with certainty— if all perspectives are equally true—then judgments about right and wrong, truth and error, correct and incorrect are purely matters of personal experience and circumstantial utility. Postmoderns adopt the view that truth is experiential. So what is true for me may not be true for you.

Given the relative nature of truth, postmodernism branches in one of two directions. It either becomes pragmatic (truth is what works in a given situation) or existential (truth is equal to my experience). As a result of the pragmatic and existential nature of truth, postmoderns are left with a truth that is always contaminated by individual interpretation and is relative to a given situation. What is true in one context is not true in another. The notion of timeless truths, truths that are true in any con-text, is unacceptable to postmodern philosophy.

The problem with relativistic truth is that it logically fails to produce a universal morality. What are left are only individual orientations to morality. The leader is unable to ever challenge an act, thought, or decision or even make a personal judgment on right or wrong, correct or incorrect.

But postmoderns do realize that the offer of absolute personal freedom from absolute truth eventually leads to chaos, despair, and anarchy. To counter this problem, postmoderns propose relative truth be determined by the tribe or community to maintain order.

TRUTH IS COMMUNAL. Communal wisdom is seen as greater and more reliable than individual wisdom. Christian postmodern theologian Stanley Grenz states his views and those of postmodernism on communal truth quite clearly. He writes,

> The idea that the world is constructed through the social conventions people bring to it leads to a decisively communal understanding of truth. Postmoderns declare that the specific truths people accept and even their understanding of truth is a function of the social group or the community in which they participate. Truth fits within a specific community; truth consists in the ground rules that facilitate the well-being of a community.
>
> The communal nature of truth results in a new kind of relativism. This new relativism is precipitated by life in social groups—or tribes— that have their own language, beliefs, and values. The older individualistic relativism elevated personal choice as the "be all" and "end all." Its maxims were: "Each to his own," and "Everyone has a right to his own opinion." Postmoderns, in contrast, tend to espouse a communal relativism that is expressed in maxims such as, "What is right for us, may not be right for you," and "What is wrong in our context, may be okay or even preferable in your context."[14]

Postmoderns embrace pluralism because of this view of truth. Pluralism is the belief that all worldviews are equally valid and rejects the concept of a metanarrative (ultimate story) that explains the meaning and purpose to life. Pluralism affirms more than just the fact that there are many different faiths and belief systems. It affirms that each of these faiths and belief systems are equally true and valid independent of any other faith or system of belief. As a result, pluralism embraces *tolerance* of all views, not as a moral action, but as the only possible means by which diverse worldviews can coexist. Besides, if one embraces postmodern thinking, on what basis can one worldview dominate any other? So exclusivity is rejected and *inclusivity* is established as the desired norm.

What does this do to a Christian worldview and to leaders who seek to communicate the exclusive claims of Christ as "the way and the truth and the life" and the exclusive claim that there is "no other name by which we may be saved"? Such a claim becomes scandalous, offensive, and arrogant. To claim that Christ is "Lord of lords" in a pluralistic world is the height of exclusivity and is arrogant in the extreme.

Impact on the Church: Truth Decay

Christian philosopher Francis Schaeffer warned the church to resist this philosophy. Ahead of his time, he saw a drift toward it that would destroy the message and effectiveness of the church.[15] Here is the danger. Many Christian leaders, in an effort to be culturally relevant, have accommodated postmodernism to the point of becoming indistinct from it. This has occurred in two basic ways. The first is the pragmatic approach to postmodernism. The second is the existentialist approach.

PRAGMATIC CHURCHES. Pragmatism is simply defining truth as "doing what works." Some churches have adopted this version of postmodern thinking. Their view could be summarized with the saying, "When in Rome, do as the Romans do." Pragmatism offers no absolutes. Instead, it seeks instrumental or utilitarian truth—truth that works in the moment. In an effort to reach as many as possible and be nonoffensive, every possible characteristic of the church that smacks of exclusivity or intolerance is removed, and the church is marketed to a postmodern society.

But many in our culture don't buy the package. One Saturday night a couple of years ago, my wife and I went to a local restaurant for dinner. It was one of those places several culinary steps above a typical fast-food restaurant with the only similarity being that you still order your food as you enter. As we considered the menu choices during our wait in line, a swarm of people entered the building. Soon the line extended all the way out the door.

New to the area, we commented to each other about the sudden interest in charbroiled hamburgers and baked potatoes. The person behind us laughed and said, "Oh, that's just Six Flags over Jesus letting out of their Saturday night service." She was referring to a megachurch in our area that draws literally thousands each week to its services. That church has a wonderful and powerful ministry in our community, and I mean no ill will in sharing this story. You see, I am certain that this church is having an enormously positive evangelistic impact, but I do think that the perception of this one woman in line at a nearby restaurant is also important. For her, there was something wrong with this picture. As we talked further, I discovered that, at least in her eyes, this church had come to look like a Christian amusement park. Based on her observations, she saw this expression of contemporary Christianity as a neatly packaged marketing plan, implemented by a corporate giant and little more. Whether her perception was accurate or not, her perspective is a challenge to Christian leaders.

One can understand her conclusions. Some of our megachurches, as they have come to be called, have footprints that look similar to the corporate headquarters of a Fortune 500 company. They are a sight to behold. Massive auditoriums, recreational facilities that make the local athletic center look like an elementary school gym, and parking lots that rival the Mall of America in number of parking spaces.

Many contemporary churches have learned the lessons of mass

marketing well. We understand why this is so. Much of, if not most of, our understanding of Christian leadership and church management is rooted firmly in the American business culture and its leadership literature. Consistent with that corporate worldview, we have come to measure churches by their size, their rate of growth, and the number of square feet in their newly constructed facility.

Church leaders have come to understand the power of branding, image creation, and targeted marketing methods. And, although the thought may not be directly spoken, as leaders we have come to reason that, "If big is the measure of ministry effectiveness, then God surely must be pleased." Please don't misunderstand me here. While these concepts have a place, they must not replace the most fundamental measure of a church and a church leader—faithfulness to teaching from the authority of Scripture and teaching its authentic expression in the life of God's people.

Since I am a staff member in a megachurch and the associate dean responsible for a doctoral program in leadership, this woman's critique of a neighboring church could have just as easily been leveled at me personally. You see, I teach Christian leaders principles of leadership—principles drawn from Scripture, to be sure, but also from the world of business, sports, the military, and the social sciences. Philosophically, I believe that "all truth is God's truth," and I heartily affirm the concept of the integration of truth from both general and special revelation in the task of Christian leadership. But this woman's humor drives me back to the most basic principle of all in biblical leadership—that being the principle of biblical authority, or *Sola Scriptura*, as the Reformation leaders have expressed it.

In one sense, this woman is right. When it comes to leadership, the church in some aspects has lost its way. Looking more like a corporate CEO than the Good Shepherd, pastoral leaders have come to define the functions of a Christian leader in terms of vision statements, purpose-driven models, church growth strategies, and motivational techniques. No longer does the proclamation or parish model[16] of ministry prevail in the minds of pastors or in their training. It has been replaced with the church as an enterprise and the pastor as entrepreneur.

Of course, all of this has occurred for good reasons. The goals have been evangelistic in nature, and who can argue with or criticize that? The desire is rightly to be culturally relevant so the largest number of people can be reached for Christ. We are driven by a harvest theology—we have seen fields that are white unto harvest and do not want to miss this unique opportunity to win lost people. That is a reasonable goal, but it is important that we are not drawn into the fallacy of pragmatic thinking in which the ends justify the means.

On this point, the emergent church movement is right. They correctly critique pragmatic tendencies in many evangelical churches. Pragmatism is an outgrowth of postmodern thinking that measures morality or success by the results of the act.

Authentic biblical leadership is not defined by result, but by faithfulness. The size of a ministry tells us little, if anything, about how God views a leader or a church. No, authentic biblical leadership is first defined by how the leader, and the ministry under that leader's care, views and responds to the Bible. Remember, it is the authority of the Word of God that is paramount to Christian leadership.

EXISTENTIALIST CHURCHES. Existentialism is a philosophy that denies universal truth around which life should be structured. Rather, it starts with life and experience and tries to determine if any truth can be discerned.

In the examination of experience, the existentialist hopes to struggle to understand the meaning of one's experience. Life is a narrative, a story, and truth is relative to that story. Truth is constructed as a way to explain experience. Experience is not aligned with self-evident or preexistent truth.

It is interesting to note that existentialist churches are often reactions to the market-driven, purpose-driven nature of pragmatic churches. Seeing the environment of the mall-like nature of the megachurch, including its food courts, coffee shops, and bowling alleys, many churches react in a pendulum fashion and go to the opposite extreme. Experience replaces a market-driven message and story replaces the "four spiritual laws." The difficulty is that if we embrace experience without any means of authenticating the validity of an experience, all experiences become equal and personal. Who then is to say what is a true and genuine experience and what is not?

THE DITCH OF CULTURAL ISOLATION

After graduating from Moody Bible Institute in Chicago, I attended a small denominational college in the southwest. At that time, Moody only offered a three-year diploma (it is now a four-year, degree-granting institution), so students had to go elsewhere to complete their degrees. Most schools required an additional two years to complete a bachelor's degree, but I found a small school of only a couple hundred students that would grant my degree in one year of further study. That sounded like a good concept to me, especially since I intended to go on to seminary. Marlene and I packed up all of our belongings and were off.

The school was what I would term a "fightin' fundamentalist" institution. It was doctrinally sound but was extremely militant in its approach to Christianity. It was interesting to sit in chapel and hear the messages preached day after day and week after week that attacked the ministry of Billy Graham, Bill Bright, and other evangelical leaders. They were "compromisers" in their attempt to reach the world, using the world's methods and failing to separate themselves from the world.

But separation from the world was not enough for the leaders of that institution. They demanded that Christians separate themselves from those who were not separated from the world, a kind of second and even third degree of separation. Taken to an extreme, their understanding of separation led to disassociation with fellow believers and a form of isolation from the world they sought to reach. They had a wonderful theology of evangelism and discipleship, but were utterly ineffective in implementing it. They knew their Bible and could spot a heretic at a hundred yards, but expressed little compassion for people in need and no empathy for those caught in the bondage of sin. It was Christ against culture for these believers, and they were His soldiers ready to do battle.

I can recall vividly when the Beatles band member, John Lennon, was shot and killed in New York City. Shortly after the news of his death, the president of that school preached on why John Lennon "had it coming" and why his death was God's retribution to him for his sin. He then preached on the ills of rock music.

As we walked out of chapel that day, several students discussed how disappointed they were in the lack of Christian charity expressed in that message. For days later students discussed the message. Several expressed that they had "had enough" and that the attitudes expressed were "not Christlike." Many decided, including me, to look to other schools for their training. Here was a school and its leadership entirely disconnected from the culture, isolated in their fortress mindset.

Today, that school is defunct. It closed for lack of students. It collapsed upon itself as the pastors it trained were equally disconnected from their culture. They led churches that were few in number and mili-tant in their relationship to the culture and even toward other Christians. The fruit they produced were small and struggling churches—not small because of their location or division, but small because of a ministry philosophy that isolated them from the lost. Those churches were typically ineffective in reaching unchurched, lost people.

Unable to sustain the school due to declining churches, churches that were closing, and students who were disenchanted with leadership, the college ceased to be. Isolation eventually brought decline and death. This was not true of the denomination as a whole though. Many leaders rejected the isolationist tendencies of the branch of the denomination represented by that school. Those churches have grown, new churches have been planted, and the schools they support have flourished.

Cultural isolationism is a ditch as deadly as the ditch of cultural accommodation. To be in the world but not of it, to be salt and light, to be known for our love for one another and the world we seek to reach are goals we cannot achieve from either ditch.

LEADING FROM THE CENTER

It is not difficult to be relevant if you don't care about being biblical. And it is not difficult to be biblical if you don't care about being relevant. The real challenge is to be both at the same time. To achieve that difficult balance leader-teachers must be students of both the Bible and students of our culture. Like Paul at Athens in Acts 17, we must present the unchanging message of Jesus in a way that is both contemporary and true to Scripture.

Leadership requires that we recognize the need for an authority beyond our own opinion or experience. To lead from the center, we must have a standard that we can depend upon. Leading from the center does not mean that we are absolutely certain about everything we think to be true. There are degrees of certainty. I can be certain that this is printed on white paper because of firsthand experience with the paper. Sure, I am dependent on my senses, but I know with certainty that in reality this paper is white. I could do an experiment and ask everyone who reads this book on what color paper the pages are printed. I am highly certain I will get far more people telling me that the pages are white rather than some other color. So I can be highly certain about some beliefs I hold.

On the other hand, I may be somewhat less certain about other beliefs. Some I believe are, in fact, only probabilities. For example, I can be certain "beyond a reasonable doubt" that Abraham Lincoln's birthplace was in Kentucky. Of course, I wasn't there for his birth and I am dependent on the scholarship of others, but I can be certain to the reasonably high degree that the evidence is weighted in that direction, that Kentucky is indeed his home state.

Leading from the center does not mean that we have no doubts or must be intolerant of those who disagree. It means that we hold some beliefs with less tenacity than others. It means that we recognize a reality separate from ourselves and that we need a standard to gauge the correctness of our perspective on that reality, acknowledging the need for authoritative and absolute truth.

We are not the standard, nor do we create truth. While we might construct our understanding of the world, our understanding is not the starting point of our leadership—God's Word is. We use the Word of God to judge the congruency between our own worldview and the real world of God's creation and design. We do not dismiss the potential of discovering truth from sources outside of the Bible, but as biblical leaders, we measure those truth claims against the clear teachings of the Bible.

Those who lead from the center recognize that there is a difference between truth and belief. Truth is not subject to my opinion, feelings, or personal beliefs. Truth corresponds to the world as it really is and is separate and distinct from my perspective.

Beliefs represent my perspectives on the truth and they may or may not be congruent with reality. The question is this: To what degree am I certain my beliefs actually correlate with what is real or true? Or, to put it another way, how confident am I that my interpretation is correct? Remember, postmoderns contend that you and I cannot know that our interpretations are in fact accurate; but leaders who lead under the authority of Scripture understand that beliefs have differing degrees of justification based on the evidence available. They also understand that because evidence can change, beliefs can change, but truth remains stable and is not dependent on belief to be true. Roderick Chisholm has produced a helpful scale to classify degree of justification of beliefs.

Table 4-1
CHISHOLM'S TRUTH CLASSIFICATION SCALE[17]

6	Certain
5	Obvious
4	Evident
3	Beyond a reasonable doubt
2	Epistemically in the clear
1	Probable
0	Counter-balanced (evidence for and against offset each other)
-1	Probably false
-2	In the clear to disbelieve
-3	Reasonable to disbelieve
-4	Evidently false
-5	Obviously false
-6	Certainly false

Leaders know that without some measure of certainty about what is true, you cannot identify what is a lie. Without authoritative truth, there can be no falsehoods, and without sound doctrine, there can be no false teachers. Biblical leaders who lead from the center do so based on authoritative truth of God's Word. Leaders who lead from the center understand the need for authority and reject the notion that because some things are less certain than others, nothing is certain. Likewise, they are not willing to hold that they are right on every point either. They do not despair, like the postmoderns, in a belief that all truth is subject to interpretation. Rather, they are discerning, recognizing that some beliefs are cardinal and others are secondary. As biblical leaders who lead from the middle, they do not allow their feelings to define their direction, for that would be a recipe for disaster as a leader.

PILOT ERROR: LEADERSHIP WITHOUT AUTHORITY

It was a pristine winter day with the sun glistening off of the newly fallen snow. I had been flying for about an hour and was turning my Cessna 172 for final approach to runway 24 at Palwaukee Municipal Airport north of Chicago. I could tell that my instructor was pleased. Though relatively new at it, I was getting the feel for flying. Moments later, I made what I thought to be a nearly perfect landing. Without comment on my landing, my instructor spoke up. "It's time to go under the hood. Yes, you definitely are ready for time under the hood." I wasn't sure to what he was referring. My first thought was he was going to show me the plane's engine. I asked him what he meant. He reached around behind him and pulled out a strange-looking device.

"We are going to take off as usual and head north away from the O'Hare traffic. Once we get to five thousand feet and forty miles from trouble, you're going to put this thing on and fly the plane," he explained. The device was designed to fit like a baseball cap but had a large shield that allowed the pilot to see only his instruments. I followed his instructions and flew out over the Illinois-Wisconsin state line. Once we were in the desired location and at the right altitude he turned to me and said, "Okay, put this on. When you do, you will not be able to see outside the plane. You will only see the controls and your instruments. Here is what I want you to remember: No matter what, trust your instruments, not your feelings."

He then took control of the plane and began to make all sorts of maneuvers. Without the ability to look out the window and see the horizon or the ground, I became disoriented. I really wasn't sure if we were turning, climbing, or descending. He began to instruct me what to do next. "Imagine you have just flown into a cloud or are trying to land in fog. Without an outside reference point, you will feel like you feel right now, disoriented. What you need to remember is to trust your instruments, not your feelings."

After several minutes of flying "under the hood," it became

apparent how important his admonition truly was. Everything in my body said I was in level flight, but the artificial horizon, an instrument that tells the pilot the orientation of his wings to the horizon, indicated that I was in a turn and descending. "If you don't trust your instruments you will enter what is known as the dead man's spiral and crash. What's worse, you will never know what hit you. That is why you must trust your instruments and not your feelings," warned my instructor.

Tragically, that is probably what happened to John F. Kennedy Jr. on July 16, 1999. John, his wife, and his sister-in-law were flying from New Jersey to Martha's Vineyard when the plane he was flying crashed into the sea. Two hours before his flight, Kennedy had gotten a weather forecast from the Internet, but it offered no caution that the haze that hung over his route could obscure a pilot's vision of the horizon. The forecast called for good visual-flying conditions with visibility of six to eight miles. It is likely that Kennedy became disoriented as he flew over the ocean on a nearly moonless night in the thick haze. Kennedy's Piper Saratoga made a series of meandering turns as it tried to approach the airport at Martha's Vineyard. At 9:41 p.m. it crashed into the Atlantic Ocean. The NTSB report later revealed that the wreckage of Kennedy's single-engine aircraft showed no evidence of a fire, no in-flight breakup, and no engine or other mechanical problems. Their conclusion? Pilot error.

In these days of postmodern uncertainty and pragmatic direction setting, biblical leaders who lead based on emotion, business trends, or cultural reference points are in danger. It is far better to "fly under the hood" of biblical authority and trust the instruments than to enter the death spiral of one's feelings or experience. Biblical leadership begins with a commitment to biblical authority.

Chapter Five

THE VIRTUOUS LEADER:
THE CHARACTER OF
THE LEADER-TEACHER

A good name is to be more desired than great riches,
Favor is better than silver and gold.

—Proverbs 22:1 (NASB)

Command and teach these things. Don't let anyone look down
on you because you are young, but set an example for the be-
lievers in speech, in life, in love, in faith and in purity. Until
I come, devote yourself to the public reading of Scripture, to
preaching and to teaching.

—1 Timothy 4:11–13

CARLETON "Carly" Fiorina, Chairman and CEO of Hewlett Packard, made the following observation in the June 2004 issue of *The Costco Connection.*

I think leadership takes, what I call, a strong internal compass. When the winds are howling and the storms are raging and the sky is cloudy so you have nothing to navigate by, a compass tells you if you're doing the right things for the right reasons in the right ways. Sometimes that's all you have.[1]

The compass that guides the biblical leader is the Word of God, and the character of God is its true north. In the last chapter we looked at the importance of a commitment to the authority of Scripture for those who seek to be effective leader-teachers. In this chapter, we will consider another foundational matter—the character of the leader-teacher. It is character that is the measure of a leader-teacher, and it is character that establishes the leader-teacher's credibility with those they seek to influence.

When leadership expert Peter Drucker died in November of 2005, the *Washington Post* described him as "the world's most influential business guru . . . whose thinking transformed corporate management in the latter half of the 20th century."[2] Drucker spoke clearly to the significance of a leader's character. He wrote of the importance of every leader conducting what he called *the mirror test*[3] and encouraged leaders to make sure that the person they see in the mirror every morning is truly the kind of person they, themselves, would want to follow. Is that person in the mirror the person they want to be, the kind of person they could respect if they were following, and the kind of person they could believe in times of crisis? He cautioned that a lack of consistency between one's public and private lives, sooner or later, would bring the demise of a leader's effectiveness.

He was correct. Leadership flows from who we are and how we express our character. This is especially the case when leadership is exercised through the vehicle of teaching.

FINDING CHARACTER: THE TRENDS IN LEADERSHIP RESEARCH

It is encouraging to note that recent leadership research affirms what biblical leaders have known ever since Jesus washed the disciples' feet and Paul called young Timothy to be an example to those he sought to teach—*character counts*. Today, a growing number of business writers are seeing the importance of character as they embrace a concept termed *servant-leadership*. Attributed first to Robert Greenleaf,[4] many other well-known and widely read authors, such as Dennis Bakke,[5] Warren Bennis,[6] Peter Block,[7] Stephen Covey,[8] Max De Pree,[9] James Kouzes,[10] Parker Palmer,[11] Tom Peters,[12] and Peter Senge,[13] have come to be staunch advocates of *servant-leadership*. By *servant-leadership* they are referring to the concept also commonly referred to as *values-based leadership*. It is a concept of leadership that emphasizes the character of the leader whose life brings respect and who places more value on the follower than on the task to be accomplished. These authors are correct in their analysis that a servant-leader—that is, a leader driven by fundamental values of character and the human worth and dignity of the follower—is essential to leadership effectiveness.

The word *character* comes from the Greek word *kharakter*, meaning "an engraver's mark or stamp." Engraver's marks were used to identify the quality of an object. We get the word *characteristic* from this same word. When we speak of a "personality characteristic," we are referring to a fundamental quality of an individual's psychological makeup. In writing, *characters* are the key players in a narrative or the letters or symbols that make up words. In all of these cases, the word *character* refers to the most basic component of something.

Similarly, *character traits* are the basic components of one's personality. It is these character traits that are the fundamental qualities that give the leader-teacher credibility. It is true that one can use raw power, coercion, deception, or manipulation to lead without character. One can even lead with charisma without possessing character. But one cannot for long be an effective biblical leader-teacher without character. It is a virtuous and godly character that provides the evidence that the content of one's teaching is indeed true and that it can be lived with authenticity.

VALUES AND VIRTUES: AN ESSENTIAL DISTINCTION

Values are crucial and servanthood is certainly the summary term for biblical leadership, but character is more than values or servanthood.

From a biblical perspective, *character is the consistent enactment of biblical values through the power of Christlike virtues.*

Values are only half the story when it comes to the leader's character. Values are principles, standards, or qualities considered worthwhile and desirable. Values are beliefs that a person or group holds and in which they have an emotional investment and heartfelt commitment. But despite the contemporary call to "values-based" leadership, assenting to a set of values—even if done wholeheartedly—is just not enough.

Here are the problems. To begin with, everyone has values. Whether they're good ones or not, we each possess values. So it is important to consider what values we are talking about and whose values we will embrace. From a biblical perspective, we must state clearly that not all values are created equal, notwithstanding what our culture may proclaim to the contrary. What's more, we all know that people can agree to the validity of a value but then not uphold that value. As imperfect humans, we often lack the power to enact our values in real-life situations.

Virtues, on the other hand, are moral excellencies and qualities of righteousness corresponding to the nature and character of God. Because virtues are drawn from the very character of God, virtues are universally morally correct. Truthfulness, wisdom, justice, compassion, love, and courage are examples of such virtues. These qualities are not right for one culture, era, or situation and wrong for another. Virtues are not relative. Virtues are the capacities of one's character that enable the leader to do the right thing even against temptation or opposition. Virtues are not external, they are internal. Virtues are part of our moral fabric producing the longing to do what is right even when there are no rewards in doing the right.

Vice President Dan Quayle brought the matter of values to American public discourse in his May 19, 1992, speech on family values. He spoke in a response to deadly and horrific rioting that had occurred in Los Angeles earlier in the month with these words. "I believe the lawless social anarchy which we saw is directly related to the breakdown of family structure, personal responsibility and social order in too many areas of our society."[14] It was his concluding statement, though, that received editorial scrutiny by the media. He said, "It doesn't help matters when prime-time TV has Murphy Brown—a character who supposedly epitomizes today's intelligent, highly paid, professional woman—mocking the importance of fathers, by bearing a child alone, and calling it just another lifestyle choice."[15] Quayle was ahead of his time in his reference to the role of values in shaping human behavior.

But even before Vice President Quayle discussed the matter of values, Margaret Thatcher had already raised the issue of values in English politics. In 1983, Margaret Thatcher, prime minister of the United Kingdom and leader of Great Britain's Conservative Party, was in a challenging election campaign. As candidates have in recent presidential campaigns in the United States, Thatcher raised the issue of moral values in one of her campaign speeches. She expressed her desire to restore "Victorian values" to Great Britain. She boldly acknowledged her longings in these words.

> The other day I appeared on a certain television program. And I was asked whether I was trying to restore "Victorian values." I said straight out, yes I was. And I am. And if you ask me whether I believe in the puritan work ethic, I'll give you an equally straight answer to that too.
>
> I believe that honesty and thrift and reliability and hard work and a sense of responsibility for your fellow men are not simply Victorian values. They do not get out of date. They are not tied to any particular place or century. You could just as well call them "Scottish Values" or "English Values." They are part of the enduring principles of the Western world. And if we just write them off and wave them goodbye, we are destroying the best of our heritage.[16]

On another occasion, in a radio interview, she specifically praised her Victorian grandmother. She stated,

I was brought up by a Victorian grandmother. You were taught to work jolly hard, you were taught to improve yourself, you were taught self-reliance, you were taught to live within your income, you were taught that cleanliness was next to godliness. You were taught self-respect, you were taught always to give a hand to your neighbor, you were taught tremendous pride in your country, you were taught to be a good member of your community. All of these things are Victorian values. They are also perennial values.[17]

With all due respect to Margaret Thatcher, who won her election, and to Dan Quayle, who lost his, it is not values that are paramount—it is *virtues*. Prime Minister Thatcher's grandmother would never have referred to these as *values*. She would have spoken of *virtues*. The term *values* is rather recent in its usage. It was not until the twentieth century that the word *values* was substituted for *virtues*. But why the shift in word usage?

The term *values* carries the assumption of moral neutrality and sub-jectivity. As the culture moved toward relativity, the word *values* took hold. That was because it described customs and conventions, not moral absolutes to which all persons must adhere. In late twentieth-century thinking, values were individualized. Each person could have their own values. Values could be race-specific, class-specific, and gender-specific. Values could be personalized to the individual, culture group, or society as each saw fit. Values could be clarified and discussed in a nonjudgmental way. By the end of the twentieth century, the term *values* became unshakably ingrained in our vocabulary. So thoroughly is the term *values* a part of our thinking that we can hardly recall a time when the term was not used. What's more, terms like *virtues* sound archaic and, well, Victorian.

But it is a virtuous character that is indispensable to the effective biblical leader. *Virtue* is a term that describes the deeper strengths of human character. In fact, it comes from the Latin word *virtus*, mean-ing power. Virtues are the power of moral goodness that brings about the achievement of one's values. Virtuous leadership is the kind of influence that comes from modeling biblical values with the power of Christlike virtues.

THE POWER OF A VIRTUOUS LEADER

It was January 30, 1956. Dr. Martin Luther King Jr. was attending a civil rights meeting at a Montgomery, Alabama, church when he received word that his house had been bombed. He rushed home and was relieved to find that no one in his family was hurt. He wrote about the incident in his book *Stride Toward Freedom.*

> I was immediately driven home. As we neared the scene I noticed hundreds of people with angry faces in front of the house. The policemen were trying, in their usual rough manner, to clear the streets, but they were ignored by the crowd. One Negro was saying to a policeman, who was attempting to push him aside: "I ain't gonna move nowhere. That's the trouble now; you white folks is always pushin' us around. Now you got your .38 and I got mine; so let's battle it out." As I walked toward the front of the porch I realized that many people were armed. Nonviolent resistance was on the verge of being transformed into violence.
>
> In this atmosphere I walked out to the porch and asked the crowd to come to order. In less than a moment there was complete silence. Quietly I told them that I was all right and that my wife and baby were all right. "Now let's not become panicky," I continued. "If you have weapons, take them home; if you do not have them, please do not seek to get them. We cannot solve this problem through retaliatory violence. We must meet violence with nonviolence. Remember the words of Jesus: 'He who lives by the sword will perish by the sword.'" I then urged them to leave peacefully. "We must love our white brothers," I said, "no matter what they do to us. We must make them know that we love them. Jesus still cries out in words that echo across the centuries:

'Love your enemies; bless them that curse you; pray for them that despitefully use you.' This is what we must live by. We must meet hate with love. Remember," I ended, "if I am stopped, this movement will not stop, because God is with the movement. Go home with this glowing faith and this radiant assurance."[18]

Someone in the crowd responded with an "Amen." Then someone else said, "God bless you." Soon the crowd dispersed and bloodshed was averted. The next day a picture of King standing on his devastated front porch and calling for a peaceful, nonviolent response hit the papers. From that moment, national support for the civil rights movement began to take hold. By his strength of character as seen in the virtues of courage, wisdom, and faith in God, King taught an entire nation from that porch that night. That night, King's credibility as a leader-teacher was established. Certainly, weaknesses of character were also present in the life of Martin Luther King Jr., but it was out of some basic virtues that his leadership flowed.

Virtue is, in itself, a kind of power or influence. In 1940, England stood alone against Hitler's blitzkrieg. The United States tried to remain neutral and had yet to enter the conflict. In less than a year, most of continental Europe was in Nazi hands, and things looked bleak for Great Britain. In what was considered England's darkest hour, Winston Churchill rallied the British people with these words:

> We shall go on to the end, we shall fight in France, we shall fight on the seas and oceans, we shall fight with growing confidence and growing strength in the air, we shall defend our Island, whatever the cost may be, we shall fight on the beaches, we shall fight on the landing grounds, we shall fight in the fields and in the streets, we shall fight in the hills; we shall never surrender, and even if, which I do not for a moment believe, this Island or a large part of it were subjugated and starving, then our Empire beyond the seas, armed and guarded by the British Fleet, would carry on the struggle, until, in God's good time, the New

World, with all its power and might, steps forth to the rescue and the liberation of the old.[19]

After the war, he said, "Never flinch, never weary, never despair. No matter how bleak the forecast, courage would carry us forward, for courage is the essential virtue because it guaranteed all the others."[20] As a man of virtue, Churchill was able to inspire and lead his people who responded to the virtue of courage so pronounced in his speeches.

A leader who leads from the virtues of his character can motivate us in powerful ways. Leader-teachers have come to understand this principle. The virtues of character are the right place to begin as a leader-teacher. After all, education should be a moral venture, so it is only logical that the leader-teacher embodies the virtues being taught. Likewise, a person who expects to teach but whose life does not match his teaching speaks with empty words and without authority. Jesus warned of this as He spoke of the hypocrisy of the Pharisees.

> Then Jesus said to the crowds and to his disciples: "The teachers of the law and the Pharisees sit in Moses' seat. So you must obey them and do everything they tell you. But do not do what they do, for they do not practice what they preach. They tie up heavy loads and put them on men's shoulders, but they themselves are not willing to lift a finger to move them." (Matthew 23:1–4)

And later, in that same chapter, Jesus said of the Pharisees,

> "Woe to you, teachers of the law and Pharisees, you hypocrites! You are like whitewashed tombs, which look beautiful on the outside but on the inside are full of dead men's bones and everything unclean. In the same way, on the outside you appear to people as righteous but on the inside you are full of hypocrisy and wickedness." (Matthew 23:27–28)

A former Pharisee himself, Paul experienced a drastic change in his character that made him a powerful and credible teacher. After an amazing transformation that began on the Damascus Road, Paul eventually became God's chosen teacher to the Gentiles (Acts 9:15). It was more than knowledge of the truth that gave Paul credibility as a teacher. God used a wide range of experiences to develop character in Paul, which he recounts in 2 Corinthians 11 and in Philippians 3:4–6. These virtue-developing experiences, along with the powerful work of the Spirit in his life, enabled Paul to state with confidence his role as virtuous leader-teacher.

> Finally, brothers, whatever is true, whatever is noble, whatever is right, whatever is pure, whatever is lovely, whatever is admirable— if anything is excellent or praiseworthy—think about such things. Whatever you have learned or received or heard from me, or seen in me—put it into practice. And the God of peace will be with you. (Philippians 4:8–9)

It was the consistency of his own life that allowed him to counsel his young protégé Timothy, with these words.

> Command and teach these things. Don't let anyone look down on you because you are young, but set an example for the believers in speech, in life, in love, in faith and in purity. Until I come, devote yourself to the public reading of Scripture, to preaching and to teaching. (1 Timothy 4:11–13)

Values are significant to the success of a leader, but it is a life that manifests godly virtue that gives the greatest credibility to the leader-teacher. Leader-teachers seek to be virtue-based leaders. While we hear and read much about the impact and importance of vision and values in leadership, these are not nearly as foundational as is a life of Christ-like virtue.

Dr. Billy Graham is an immediate and obvious example of this fact.

Clearly, he was visionary and there is no doubt about his values. But what is most striking about Dr. Graham is his virtuous leadership. Known as a man of "profound humility" and "utmost integrity," Dr. Graham understood the importance of being a person of deep character convictions. He once said, "When wealth is lost, nothing is lost. When health is lost, something is lost. When character is lost, all is lost."[21]

There are plenty of examples of character failure in both biblical and contemporary times for us to see the impact of this failure on both the leaders and their followers. Success is not a sufficient foundation on which the leader-teacher can build a teaching ministry. At the core must be a commitment to the Scriptures as authority over all of life, including the personal life and character of the leader-teacher.

THE VIRTUES OF THE LEADER-TEACHER

If you ask people to identify a leader, they will often name a person with a charismatic personality. But charisma is really not the primary quality of biblical leadership. *At the heart of biblical leadership is the leader's heart.*

Biblical Virtues of Leadership

As Paul worked to establish churches, he also addressed the need for leaders in those churches. He was concerned for the well-being of those churches, so he appointed elders or leaders to shepherd each fledgling flock. These leaders were to be selected primarily on their virtuous character, because godly character is the surest outward indicator of the work of the Spirit of God in a leader's life. In two of the Pastoral Epistles, we find detailed lists of the qualifications of these elders. These lists are similar but not identical because the needs of the church at Ephesus (1 Timothy 3) were quite different from those at Crete (Titus 1). What they share in common is a focus on the character of the leader as the dominant qualifying factor for those who would lead the church. Take a moment and read the passages below. Notice the focus in each on the character of the elder.

QUALIFICATIONS OF ELDERS

1 Timothy 3:1–7	Titus 1:5–9
Here is a trustworthy saying: If anyone sets his heart on being an overseer, he desires a noble task. Now the overseer must be above reproach, the husband of but one wife, temperate, self-controlled, respectable, hospitable, able to teach, not given to drunkenness, not violent but gentle, not quarrelsome, not a lover of money. He must manage his own family well and see that his children obey him with proper respect. (If anyone does not know how to manage his own family, how can he take care of God's church?) He must not be a recent convert, or he may become conceited and fall under the same judgment as the devil. He must also have a good reputation with outsiders, so that he will not fall into disgrace and into the devil's trap.	The reason I left you in Crete was that you might straighten out what was left unfinished and appoint elders in every town, as I directed you. An elder must be blameless, the husband of but one wife, a man whose children believe and are not open to the charge of being wild and disobedient. Since an overseer is entrusted with God's work, he must be blameless—not overbearing, not quick-tempered, not given to drunkenness, not violent, not pursuing dishonest gain. Rather he must be hospitable, one who loves what is good, who is self-controlled, upright, holy and disciplined. He must hold firmly to the trustworthy message as it has been taught, so that he can encourage others by sound doctrine and refute those who oppose it.

In the 1 Timothy 3 list, leaders are to be "above reproach." In the Titus passage, they are to be "blameless." Though different Greek words are used, the terms are synonymous. They speak of personal holiness. They describe the reputation of a leader. To be described as above reproach or blameless does not mean that the leader is perfect or without flaws. It means that a leader is one with a reputation whose words are supported by his or her life. A leader-teacher must have and maintain a good name. There should be no question as to his integrity or upright character. King Solomon put it poetically when he said, "A good name is more desirable than great riches, to be esteemed is better than silver and gold" (Proverbs 22:1).

John Calvin explained the concept of being above reproach in this way:

> An elder "ought not to be marked by any disgrace that would detract from his authority. There will certainly not be found a man who is free from every fault, but it is one thing to be burdened with ordinary faults that do not hurt a man's reputation, because the most excellent men share them, but quite another to have a name that is held in infamy and besmirched by some scandalous disgrace. Thus, in order that the bishops may not lack authority, he gives charge that those who are chosen should be of good and honorable reputation, and free of any extraordinary fault. Also, he is not merely directing Timothy as to the sort of men he should choose but he is reminding all who aspire to the office that they should carefully examine their own life." [22]

These phrases, "above reproach" and "blameless," serve as the summary terms for all that follow in these lists. What does it mean to the leader-teacher to be above reproach? It means that the leader-teacher has a reputation that supports their teaching ministry. Those who are called to feed and lead the people of God through teaching the Word of God, must themselves have a godly character, for a reproachful character undermines even the most competent of Bible teachers.

Several other passages identify virtues that should mark the Christian. Scripture provides a number of character profiles for leaders. Two passages in particular, Colossians 3:1–17 and Galatians 5:16–26, should be noted by the leader-teacher. One of these passages stresses the responsibility of the believer in developing moral virtues while the other stresses the work of the Holy Spirit in this process.

Colossians 3:1–17	Galatians 5:16–26
Since, then, you have been raised with Christ, set your hearts on things above, where Christ is seated at the right hand of God. Set your minds on things above, not on earthly things. For you died, and your life is now hidden with Christ in God. When Christ, who is your life, appears, then you also will appear with him in glory.	So I say, live by the Spirit, and you will not gratify the desires of the sinful nature.
	For the sinful nature desires what is contrary to the Spirit, and the Spirit what is contrary to the sinful nature. They are in conflict with each other, so that you do not do what you want. But if you are led by the Spirit, you are not under law.
Put to death, therefore, whatever belongs to your earthly nature: sexual immorality, impurity, lust, evil desires and greed, which is idolatry. Because of these, the wrath of God is coming. You used to walk in these ways, in the life you once lived. But now you must rid yourselves of all such things as these: anger, rage, malice, slander, and filthy language from your lips. Do not lie to each other, since you have taken off your old self with its practices and have put on the new self, which is being renewed in knowledge in the image of its Creator. Here there is no Greek or Jew, circumcised or uncircumcised, barbarian, Scythian, slave or free, but Christ is all, and is in all.	The acts of the sinful nature are obvious: sexual immorality, impurity and debauchery; idolatry and witchcraft; hatred, discord, jealousy, fits of rage, selfish ambition, dissensions, factions and envy; drunkenness, orgies, and the like. I warn you, as I did before, that those who live like this will not inherit the kingdom of God.
Therefore, as God's chosen people, holy and dearly loved, clothe yourselves with compassion, kindness, humility, gentleness and patience. Bear with each other and forgive whatever grievances you may have against one another. Forgive as the Lord forgave you. And over all these virtues put on love, which binds them all together in perfect unity.	But the fruit of the Spirit is love, joy, peace, patience, kindness, goodness, faithfulness, gentleness and self-control. Against such things there is no law. Those who belong to Christ Jesus have crucified the sinful nature with its passions and desires. Since we live by the Spirit, let us keep in step with the Spirit. Let us not become conceited, provoking and envying each other.
Let the peace of Christ rule in your hearts, since as members of one body you were called to peace. And be thankful. Let the word of Christ dwell in you richly as you teach and admonish one another with all wisdom, and as you sing psalms, hymns and spiritual songs with gratitude in your hearts to God. And whatever you do, whether in word or deed, do it all in the name of the Lord Jesus, giving thanks to God the Father through him.	

The Colossians passage offers motivation to godliness in the work of Christ (3:1) and in the relationship the believer has to that work. He says, "For you died, and your life is now hidden with Christ in God. When Christ, who is your life, appears, then you also will appear with him in glory" (3:3–4). This intimate relationship with the person and work of Christ calls the believer to a life consistent with the character of Christ.

This motivation demands a decisive action on the part of those who seek to be like Christ. We are called to "set [our] hearts on things above" and to "set [our] minds on things above" (3:1–2). We are to "put to death . . . whatever belongs to your earthly nature" (3:5). We are told to "rid yourselves of all such things" (3:8). We are then invited to "put on the new self " (3:10) and to "clothe yourselves" with a number of virtues, the most significant being love (3:12–14). Clearly, Paul believes there are decisions of the will and behavioral actions that Christians can take to develop godly virtues. At the same time, he is equally clear in the Galatians passage that the most basic qualities of godliness are the supernatural work of the Holy Spirit in the believer's life. So then, as theologians would state it, sanctification is a joint venture between the person of the Holy Spirit and the individual who yields his or her life to God.

It is uncommon for a single individual to demonstrate the entire list of virtues above. We are each at differing stages of development of any one virtue. Someone will greatly exhibit patience, while another greatly demonstrates kindness. Collectively, though, the church should be building itself up in all of these virtues with leader-teachers standing as authentic examples of that growth process. An individual, after many years of spiritual growth, may exhibit these traits in abundance, but it is still a process that the Holy Spirit has yet to complete.

In September 2004, my father was gravely ill. As he appeared to be near death, our family gathered at the home of my brother. A recipient of hospice care, my father lay in a hospital bed in the living room. Together our family shared our fondest memories of my dad, a very godly man with a meek spirit. My youngest son, Michael, made a comment to me that underscored the power of a godly example. Michael said, "Dad, you know the passage in the Bible that lists the fruit of the Spirit?" I nodded in reply and he continued. "Well, I think Grandpa Bredfeldt has every one of those fruits in his life." Being a man a grandson could look up to as Christlike is my father's gift and legacy to our family.

I should tell you that, by God's grace, my dad recovered from that brush with death. Though he is limited to life in a nursing home and is wheelchair bound, God continues to bless us with his always-optimistic spirit and godly joy to the day these words were written.

Classical Virtues of Leadership

Aristotle offered a now-classic list of virtues that are helpful and summative of the virtues necessary in the life of a leader-teacher. His list included seven key virtues of character—virtues still regarded as fundamental to leadership by many organizations and authors today. His list includes courage, faithfulness, hope, love, wisdom, justice, and temperance. Though not exhaustive, these traits are certainly in concert with Scripture.

LEADER-TEACHERS NEED TO BE COURAGEOUS. The English word *courage* is rooted in *coeur*, French for "heart." To have courage is to have the heart for something. To lose courage is to lose heart. Courage is the ability to overcome fear and to take action. Courage is seen in the leader-teachers who overcome personal fears and are willing to take risks, take a stand on an issue, or take command in a situation that demands that someone act. Such courage gives confidence to followers as their leaders act with composure in moments of uncertainty. Courage brings credibility to the leader-teacher and motivates the heart of the follower. To *encourage* simply means "to instill courage in another." That happens most powerfully when leaders exhibit courage themselves.

None of us will ever forget the horrific events of September 11, 2001. We watched in disbelief, outrage, and fear as aircraft were used to attack our country. Two slammed into the World Trade Center Towers in New York City, one took aim at the Pentagon in Washington DC, and the fourth, likely bound for the Capitol Building or the White House, was forced to the ground by courageous passengers who thwarted the hijackers' goal.

We were uncertain as to what might come next. But the recovery workers who dug through the Trade Tower ruins, as well as every person watching on television, were encouraged when President Bush took a megaphone in hand, put an arm around a firefighter, and then boldly called us all to be courageous as in a time of war. His strength and courage gave the country a renewed sense of power over the situation at hand. Some may have too quickly forgotten that day, but it was indeed the strength of a courageous leader, heard in his words of encouragement, that renewed the courage of a nation.

It takes courage to lead. It likewise takes courage to be a leader-teacher. Teaching brings fear. In fact, much of the educational experience has a good measure of fear for both the teacher and the learner. Teachers fear being asked questions they cannot answer, making statements they cannot support, not knowing their content thoroughly, or attempting teaching methodologies that fail. Learners fear that they will make public statements that miss the point or sound uninformed. They fear not understanding the material on which they will be evaluated. Courageous teachers both overcome their own fears and aid students in overcoming their fears as well.

LEADER-TEACHERS NEED TO BE FAITHFUL. To be a faithful person is to be a trustworthy individual. Faithfulness is foundational to effectiveness as a leader-teacher. Paul instructed Timothy and Titus with regard to elders that they be "the husband of but one wife" (1 Timothy 3:2; Titus 1:6). This phrase literally means, "a one-woman man" and is a reference to marital faithfulness. Why raise the issue of marital faithfulness with regard to a leader? It is because it is a basic measure of the trustworthiness of a leader. After all, if a leader cannot be trusted in the most fundamental of relationships, his marriage, can a leader be trusted to lead the church? Our culture has often claimed that one's private life has nothing to do with one's public role as a leader, but Scripture is clear that such a relationship does exist. You see, faithfulness to a marriage is an indicator of the depth of a man or woman's character. The virtuous leader must be someone who is trustworthy and faithful.

One aspect of faithfulness is *reliability*. People who are reliable are people you can count on. They follow through on promises, they communicate information that is accurate, and they carry out the tasks that are their duty. When it comes to communicating the truth of the Word of God, Paul instructed Timothy with these words: "And the things you have heard me say in the presence of many witnesses *entrust to reliable men* who will also be qualified to teach others" (2 Timothy 2:2, italics added). Teaching God's Word is a holy trust, requiring reliable persons, that is, faithful individuals, who will carry out that trust with competence.

Yet another facet of faithfulness is *trust*. Leader-teachers must build trust if they are to have an impact as teachers. Without trust, they simply become transmitters of information. How does a leader-teacher build trust? Terry Pearce, author of *Leading Out Loud*, suggests that you build trust by being authentic.[23] Authenticity involves being open, honest, vulnerable, and genuine. People have to know that you are the "real McCoy." Nothing breaks trust faster than phoniness.

In their book *The Trusted Leader*, Robert Galford and Anne Drapeau identify four key actions that develop trust. First, the leader must be a reliable source of information and expertise. Second, trusted leaders establish genuine personal relationships with their followers. Third, trust comes when leaders place personal interests second to those of the follower. Finally, and most important in the list, leaders gain trust by being reliable, meaning being a dependable and consistent person.[24]

LEADER-TEACHERS NEED TO BE HOPEFUL. Hope is fundamental to the character of the leader-teacher. Hope is not wishful thinking; hope is a confidence that a better outcome is possible. Hope is what gives leaders their sense of vision for the future. Visionary leaders are the embodiment of hope. Hope is the drive that causes us to press on until we attain the future.

Biblical hope springs from a confidence in God and His Word. Scripture is replete with passages addressing hope, such as Romans 12:12, "Be joyful in hope" and Romans 15:13, " . . . overflow with hope." The English word *hope* is translated from the Greek word *elpis*, meaning a *confident expectation*. It is not a vague, "Well, I hope so," but a *firm assurance* that enables the child of God to *confidently* face the context in which we live. It provides a deep sense of spiritual stability, because it is a *firm expectation* that God will keep His Word.

Hopeful leader-teachers are visionaries. They are not mired in the present. They see a future where God is doing a great work. They see students who, though at the moment may be struggling, will be able to succeed and do great things.

Hope-filled leader-teachers are optimists. J. Oswald Sanders said it wonderfully: "Vision includes optimism and hope. A pessimist sees difficulty in every opportunity. An optimist sees opportunity in every difficulty."[25] The most effective leaders are those who find meaning in difficult experiences and who face adversity with confidence and hope. Warren Bennis and Robert Thomas have reported "our recent research has led us to conclude that the most reliable indicator of true leadership is the individual's ability to find meaning in negative events and to learn from the most trying circumstances. Put another way, the skills required to conquer adversity and emerge stronger and more committed than ever are the same ones that make extraordinary leaders."[26] Despite the challenges, leader-teachers have the tendency to believe every student can reach greatness and every follower can succeed.

LEADER-TEACHERS NEED TO BE LOVING. Leader-teachers must develop hearts of compassion and a willingness to care profoundly about those they serve. Leader-teachers need a genuine, heartfelt concern for the needs, feelings, and aspirations of those they lead. But loving people does not always mean embracing their foibles. It can mean being directly honest, being confrontational, or even exercising discipline in the lives of the persons we love. Leader-teachers who truly love their students understand the varied ways that Christian love must be expressed. They know that "the Lord disciplines those he loves, and he punishes everyone he accepts as a son" (Hebrews 12:6).

Leader-teachers need to develop the virtue of love. Love is marked by a number of characteristics. 1 Corinthians 13:4–8 provides a poetic listing of the qualities of love.

> Love is patient, love is kind. It does not envy, it does not boast, it is not proud. It is not rude, it is not self-seeking, it is not easily angered, it keeps no record of wrongs. Love does not delight in evil but rejoices with the truth. It always protects, always trusts, always hopes, always perseveres. Love never fails.

Genuine love is selfless. It places the needs of the one loved first. This kind of love was demonstrated by Christ who gave His life for those He called "the sheep."

> "I am the good shepherd. The good shepherd lays down his life for the sheep. The hired hand is not the shepherd who owns the sheep. So when he sees the wolf coming, he abandons the sheep and runs away. Then the wolf attacks the flock and scatters it. The man runs away because he is a hired hand and cares nothing for the sheep. I am the good shepherd; I know my sheep and my sheep know me—just as the Father knows me and I know the Father—and I lay down my life for the sheep." (John 10:11–15)

Virtuous leader-teachers serve as undershepherds. They are called to care for and protect the sheep. That means that they must be willing to sacrificially love those they are called to serve. In Colossians, Paul identifies a list of virtues that he links to the virtue of love.

> Clothe yourselves with compassion, kindness, humility, gentleness and patience. Bear with each other and forgive whatever grievances you may have against one another. Forgive as the Lord forgave you. And over all these virtues put on love, which binds them all together in perfect unity. (Colossians 3:12–14)

James E. Means underscores the importance of this virtue for the success or failure of local church ministry. He writes,

> Effective leadership, genuine ministry, and church harmony all begin in the leadership selection process. If the church chooses mature, godly, compassionate, and gracious leaders, effective ministry and healthy growth are likely.[27]

If God has called you to be a leader-teacher, then you must seek to pattern your leadership in the manner consistent with Christ. You are to lead in both truth and righteousness, and you are to love sacrificially. Your love must make you willing to battle the savage wolves, which seek to destroy the flock, and you must be genuinely willing to lay down your life for those you lead.

Thirteenth-century monk Francis of Assisi offered a now-famous prayer that captures the essence of biblical love.

> Where there is hatred, let me sow love;
> Where there is injury, pardon;
> Where there is doubt, faith;
> Where there is despair, hope;
> Where there is darkness, light;
> And where there is sadness, joy;
> Grant that I might not so much seek to be consoled as to console;
> To be understood, as to understand;
> To be loved as to love;
> For it is in giving that we receive;
> It is in pardoning that we are pardoned.[28]

LEADER-TEACHERS NEED TO BE WISE. Leader-teachers must develop wisdom. Wisdom is the ability to discern or judge what is true, right, or lasting. Wisdom is not intelligence or knowledge. Wisdom is the application of knowledge and experience in solving real-world problems. The book of Proverbs underscores the importance and value of genuine wisdom.

> Blessed is the man who finds wisdom, the man who gains understanding, for she is more profitable than silver and yields better returns than gold. She is more precious than rubies; nothing you desire can compare with her. Long life is in her right hand; in her left hand are riches and honor. Her ways are pleasant ways, and all her paths are peace. She is a tree of life to those who embrace her; those who lay hold of her will be blessed. (Proverbs 3:13–18)

According to the Bible there are two kinds of wisdom. James, in his epistle writes,

> If you harbor bitter envy and selfish ambition in your hearts, do not boast about it or deny the truth. Such "wisdom" does not come down from heaven but is earthly, unspiritual, of the devil. For where you have envy and selfish ambition, there you find disorder and every evil practice. But the wisdom that comes from heaven is first of all pure; then peace-loving, considerate, submissive, full of mercy and good fruit, impartial and sincere. (James 3:14–17)

Worldly wisdom is characterized by jealousy, self-centered ambition, and self-promoting at the expense of others. James says that such wisdom is "earthly, unspiritual and of the devil." It is a wisdom that breeds every form of evil and advances a commitment to self over the needs of others.

Godly wisdom, on the contrary, produces purity, peace, a gentle response, a reasonableness, and the good fruits of impartiality and sincerity. These are the marks of the wise leader-teacher. There is a depth to this kind of leader that goes far beyond charisma or authoritarian power. There is a magnetism of spirituality as a leader-teacher exercises this kind of wisdom. It might seem beyond our reach to be a leader who reflects godly wisdom, but we can be encouraged by James's reminder that, "If any of you lacks wisdom, he should ask God, who gives generously to all without finding fault, and it will be given to him" (James 1:5).

LEADER-TEACHERS NEED TO BE JUST. In Titus 1:8, we are told that leaders must be "upright." Justice means being "on the level" with people and treating people fairly. The word used here is the Greek term *dikaios*. Literally, the word means to be *straight*. It describes someone who seeks to do that which is right, and who seeks to be straight with others. It involves keeping a standard and playing by the rules. A just leader is someone who is fair and honest. He or she does not manipulate, mislead, or take ethical shortcuts.

Justice is a power issue. If we use intimidation or fear to lead, we will almost always cease to be just in our dealings with others. Justice is a virtue by which we determine to do what is right. It is a moral quality or habit that inclines us to render to each person what belongs to them. When Jesus was asked whether or not taxes should be paid to Caesar, He made a statement that goes to the principle of justice. He said we should "Render to Caesar the things that are Caesar's; and to God the things that are God's" (Matthew 22:21, NASB). That is the essence of justice. Justice involves a dedication to the fair treatment of others.

We all know what it is like to be cheated. Maybe someone owes you a debt they did not pay, or you were a victim of a scam. Once I worked a number of hours only to find that I was not to be paid for the service I rendered. My feelings were frustration and anger. Eventually, I was able to surrender those feelings to God as the One who ultimately is responsible for justice, but I remember the feeling of being violated and mistreated. That experience erected a barrier that made the other person's words less credible. "Fool me once, shame on you; fool me twice, shame on me," the old saying goes.

What happens when we fail to practice justice with others? A breakdown of trust occurs. Robert Putman stresses the importance of trust to leadership and societal relationship. "A society that relies on generalized reciprocity is more efficient than a distrustful society, for the same reason that money is more efficient than barter. Honesty and trust lubricate the inevitable frictions of social life."[29] Without just treatment, people lose trust in their leaders. Once trust is lost, followers become hesitant to take risks and begin to doubt the veracity of the leader's words. When leader-teachers fail to be just, they lose what is their most valued strength in teaching—the power of their word.

LEADER-TEACHERS NEED TO BE TEMPERATE. Temperance is wisdom applied to one's own life. Temperate leaders exercise self-control and personal discipline. Paul says that an elder must be "temperate, self-controlled, respectable" (1 Timothy 3:2). Self-discipline enables us to achieve great things and avoid great pain. Self-discipline is the ability to take action regardless of our emotional state or personal desires. The word *temperance* means "moderation, balance, self-control; to regulate, manage, and to temper." According to Thomas Aquinas, the reason the leader needs temperance is to "govern the passions."[30] Governing the passions requires self-discipline.

My son Steve is the most self-disciplined individual I know. When he decides to do something, there is no halfway. Once when he was in elementary school, fourth grade I think, a basketball coach told his team, "Carbonated drinks will slow you down." The coach advised his players to stop drinking soft drinks for the rest of the season. Steve heard him loud and clear. As an athlete, Steve has always sought to be a top performer. From that day until the present, Steve has not touched a carbonated beverage. That is self-discipline. I have always said that if I had 10 percent of his self-discipline I would never have to worry about gaining or losing weight again!

Self-discipline is painful, but it is also productive. Without it, little can be achieved in leadership. Leaders who lack discipline in their own lives usually fail at the task of teaching. What is worse, they often bring others down with them in their failure. Identify anything you desire to accomplish, any goal you would like to achieve. Without self-discipline, that intention will only be a good intention and will never become reality. But with sufficient self-discipline, it can be achieved. The key to temperance is making a conscious decision and then following through on it.

Here is the good news. Even self-discipline is not wholly dependent on yourself! Remember the Galatians 5 passage we read earlier. Self-control is a fruit of the Spirit. It is a product of God's work in our lives. So again, this virtue of leadership is a joint venture with God Himself. It is a habit learned by practice and it is manifestation of God in our lives as we walk in the power of the Holy Spirit.

Self-discipline is the result of habitual use. It is like a muscle in your body. The more you train it, the stronger you become. Likewise, the less you train it, the weaker you will become. As a leader-teacher, you will have to learn to say no to yourself at times. You will need to remain disciplined in your study of God's Word. You will need to remain faithful in your walk with Christ. You will need to remain faithful to your spouse and be a reliable parent. You will need to faithfully spend time with those you seek to teach. All of these will demand a measure of self-discipline. You will especially need to develop self-discipline as you watch over your heart.

DEVELOPING A VIRTUOUS CHARACTER

It is easy to talk about virtues and far more challenging to develop them. But it can be done. Remember our word *character?* You will recall that it came from a word meaning *to engrave.* What that tells us is that character is *formed* as a process. Certainly, information and knowledge are important to character development, but for the most part, character is "engraved or notched in" to our being through the decisions and experiences of life. So, assuming you are alive as you read this, God, with your partnership, can develop character virtues in you as you seek to walk in His Spirit.

It will not be an easy process. In fact, it may require some sacrifice and pain on your part, but the end result is far greater influence and a more credible ministry. But you could not undertake a more important process. As Proverbs 22:1 says, "A good name is more desirable than great riches; to be esteemed is better than silver or gold." How can that be? Keep in mind that our character stays with us always, but power, wealth, and fame are fleeting.

It takes both character and competence to lead God's people. In Psalm 78:72 we read, "And David shepherded them with integrity of heart (character); with skillful hands he led them (competence)." In the next chapter we will deal with the matter of the competencies of the leader-teacher.

Chapter Six

WITH SKILLFUL HANDS:
THE COMPETENCIES OF THE LEADER-TEACHER

And David shepherded them with integrity of heart; with skillful hands he led them.

—Psalm 78:72

AS we saw in the previous chapter, a leader of virtuous character is essential. However, a virtuous character in itself is not enough. A leader must be competent for, or capable of doing, the tasks required. In this chapter we will discuss eight foundational competencies of the leader-teacher.

Consider a competent leader who lacks character. In such a case the risk is that a despot will arise and act in ways that strip human beings of their dignity, value, rights, and freedoms. Competence without character can lead to bad leadership.

But what about an incompetent leader who is a person of high moral integrity? In this case, the leader is of exemplary character; but without competence, an inertia and lethargy occurs. Bad leaders, then, can simply be good people who are incompetent for the task. The case of Union general Ambrose Burnside stands as a striking example of ineffectual leadership in the hands of an incompetent leader with a sterling character.

Ambrose Burnside was a 38-year-old West Point graduate appointed in 1862 by President Abraham Lincoln to lead the Army of the Potomac. Burnside commanded the Union army against General Robert E. Lee at what became one of the bloodiest battles in American history, the Battle of Fredericksburg. What is most distressing is that Burnside's command at the Battle of Fredericksburg was a testament to such incompetent leadership that it provoked a full-scale congressional investigation.

Known to be a man of deep moral conviction with an amiable and gregarious personality, Burnside was respected as a virtuous leader. His chestnut eyes and strong jaw gave him a warm and sensitive quality that attracted people to him. But he was a leader with a fatal flaw—he was incompetent as a military strategist. No amount of character, charm, or wit could atone for his inability to competently lead.

Burnside arrived at the banks of the placid Rappahannock River across from the town of Fredericksburg, Virginia, on November 19, 1862. His mission was to cross the river and take the strategic town, considered the gateway to the Confederate capital of Richmond. When Burnside arrived, the last leaves of autumn were falling from the trees, the air was still warm, and the river was low.

With 130,000 troops, Burnside outnumbered his enemy three to one. But instead of striking immediately, Burnside delayed. He was awaiting the delivery of pontoons to build bridges instead of wading across the river. So his army remained encamped on the north side of the Rappahannock.

The days passed and the pontoons finally arrived. Still Burnside did not attack. Unaccountably, Burnside allowed November to pass to December before he finally took action. But by that time the winter rains had come, the river rose to ten feet, and the currents turned swift. The edge of the river became ice covered, and crossing became far more difficult.

Burnside's delay in attacking was costly. It gave General Lee ample time to locate sharpshooters in the row homes that lined the narrow streets of the town and to locate his heavy cannons on the hills rising to the west of town. Astonished by Burnside's quick and early arrival at the river, Lee immediately moved 75,000 men to the city, a task made easy by Burnside's hesitancy to act.

With winter closing in quickly, Burnside finally had to attack. He summoned his commanders to present his plan. He would launch a series of direct frontal assaults, one after another until the town was taken. At the meeting, one brigade commander warned Burnside directly, "If you make the attack as contemplated, it will be the greatest slaughter of the war; there isn't infantry enough in our whole army to carry those heights if they are well defended."[1] With boldness, a colonel added, "The carrying out of your plan will be murder, not warfare."[2] He was correct. It was a bloodbath.

Under fire, Burnside's engineers set up the pontoon bridges, and on December 11, 1862, Federal troops crossed the river, invading Fredericksburg. After the crossing they had to run another hundred yards through a rising marsh and meadows before reaching the edge of town. It was an insane, suicidal effort. Although a fog hung over the river on the morning of the 11th, the Confederates could hear the sound of mules, wagons, and men as they tried to cross the swiftly moving river. The Union troops were mercilessly fired upon. Only by sheer force of numbers, the Union army took the town.

Then Burnside ordered an attack on Marye's Heights, the high ground where Lee's army was entrenched. Wave after wave of Union troops were mowed down. Finally, after a day of assaults, Burnside assembled his commanders and announced yet another frontal attack, which he would personally lead. But his commanders refused; there on the battlefield, in defiance, they told him there would be no more charges.

Though they took the town, the Army of the Potomac, under Burnside, suffered a costly defeat with a loss of 12,653 men after fourteen unwise frontal assaults on well-entrenched rebels on Marye's Heights. The battles were so furious and devastating to morale that a Union soldier remarked, "We might as well have tried to take hell."[3]

Burnside was a man of upstanding character who simply could not lead. At least, he lacked the competence necessary to lead in the context of battle. The essence of balanced and effective leadership is found in this simple principle: Character must be accompanied by competence. Leader-teachers must possess eight fundamental competencies to effectively achieve their leadership calling.

EIGHT COMPETENCIES OF THE LEADER-TEACHER

In both leadership and educational literature, the skill sets necessary for effectiveness in achieving any task are termed "competencies." A *competency* has been defined as "a qualification or fitness to perform an act."[4] Eight such competencies mark the effective leader-teacher. Four of these relate to the teaching aspect of the leader-teacher's calling, and four relate to the leader aspect of that calling. Together they give strength to leadership just as fence posts support and strengthen a fence. They are foundational abilities every leader-teacher must hone. The chart below summarizes these for us.

Table 6-1
EIGHT BASIC COMPETENCIES OF THE LEADER-TEACHER

TEACHER COMPETENCIES	LEADER COMPETENCIES
Message that is clear	Establish the team
Methods that promote learning	Equip the team
Model the message	Empower the team
Minister to people	Encourage the team

The Competencies of the Teacher

Great teachers are known for doing a few things extremely well. Both biblical data and empirical research support the important role of each of the following teaching skills.

MESSAGE THAT IS CLEAR. The best teachers know exactly what they want to communicate. They are driven by a set of ideas and values they want others to understand and embrace. They are confident that those ideas and values are crucial and so they communicate them with passion and clarity. Noel M. Tichy calls this "a teachable point of view."[5] Tichy explains a teachable point of view as "a cohesive set of ideas and concepts that a person is able to articulate clearly to others. The difference between a solo player and a world-class leader is the ability to teach others."[6]

Without the ability to articulate that "teachable point of view," leaders will fail to communicate and will fail to develop others. Leaders must be able to communicate their message. That ability requires a clear and precise focus.

I recently bought a camera. It is a digital model made by a highly regarded manufacturer. What sold me on this camera was a feature called "image stablization." Image stablization removes the blur you get if your hands are not steady or if the object you're shooting is moving. The result is an extremely sharp picture because "focus" is retained even when circumstances are challenging.

In both photography and teaching, *focus* is critical. In photography, focus brings clarity to a visual image. In teaching, focus brings clarity to verbal concepts. Effective leader-teachers are able to bring focus to their message through the use of precise language, intelligible thought patterns, and the use of words pregnant with meaning. Haddon Robinson calls this communicating the "big idea."[7] In *Creative Bible Teaching,* my coauthor, Larry Richards, and I provide detailed help in how to develop and state the big idea in teaching the Bible.[8]

Political advisers, public relations consultants, and advertising researchers will tell you rightly, "effective communication begins with a clear message." Poor communication most often is the result of a message that is obscure or poorly worded. Consider these real-life advertisements:

- Dinner Special: Turkey $7.95, Chicken or Beef $6.25, Children $2.00.
- Stock up and save. Limit: one per customer.
- Semiannual after-Christmas Sale
- Auto Repair Service. Free pick up and delivery. Try us once, you'll never go anywhere else again.

As humorous as these ads are they illustrate the problem of a lack of clarity in a message. *A message is a statement that resonates with your audience and compels them to act.* Leader-teachers need to be able to state their message in ways that are memorable and effective. What makes a message effective? I believe four qualities of the message are key.

First, the message must appeal logically and emotionally to the audience. Second, it must connect to the overall strategy and purpose of the group or organization being led. Third, it must be validated by evidence (e.g., Scripture, statistics, facts, anecdotes, etc.). And fourth, the language used to communicate the message must be understood by the audience. Competent leader-teachers must develop the skills of a communicator by learning to develop a *message that is clear.*

METHODS THAT PROMOTE LEARNING. Great leader-teachers use various methods to promote deeper levels of thinking, learning, understanding, and visioning of the future. They do not simply rely on didactic styles of instruction where learning is preprocessed by the teacher and simply delivered to the student. Instead they use methods that are multidimensional, inviting the hearers to use their imagination. Their teaching communicates through means that include memorable images, images bolstered by analogy, metaphor, story, and other figurative devices. These methods allow those being led to connect with the concepts being taught.

Consider for a moment an example from the archives of NASA. In 1992, Daniel Goldin, a NASA administrator, was seeking congressional backing for the concept of sending a human explorer to Mars. His goal was to motivate funding, so he chose to use an analogy to illustrate his message. He told the story of the voyages of Columbus and other explorers. He explained how only Spain's Queen Isabella had the foresight to fund such efforts and how her vision turned Spain into a world power. He explained how the language and culture of Spain spread and prevailed when these explorers ventured forth.

He then told of a very different story and a very different result. He contrasted Spain's visionary approach with China's isolationism. Some sixty years before Columbus, Chinese explorers reached Africa and were poised to travel still farther. If they had continued, they would have reached the New World long before Columbus was even born. But their quests came to an abrupt halt. Why? Because the Chinese emperor considered such journeying to be wasteful and extravagant. He saw no value in the expeditions and so he ordered the boats of explorers burned and those who would try to venture forth to worlds beyond China, executed. The result was that China became cut off, and even to this day, struggles to be fully connected to world affairs.[9]

Goldin's analogy communicated powerfully. The connection between progress and exploration was clear. He gained his funding for the Mars effort. A human being walking on Mars is a goal yet to be accomplished, but it is one that has begun as a result of the communication skills of a leader-teacher.

What does it take to be a great leader-teacher? What methodological skills must the leader-teacher develop in order to communicate ideas effectively? I would suggest four essential methods that you should invest time developing. Again, Larry Richards and I deal with these more extensively in our book *Creative Bible Teaching*,[10] so I will not go into detail here. The four key methods of the leader-teacher are:

1. STORYTELLING: Leader-teachers need to learn the skill of storytelling because stories are the universal means of teaching. Stories cause listeners to shift into what I call story-mode. Story-mode is seen when listeners move forward in their seats and even lean into the speaker to focus their concentration.

We humans love stories. They engage us.

Storytelling is the ability to relate past experiences, either real or fictional, in a way that exemplifies the big idea you desire to communicate by bringing an experience alive for the listeners. Whether telling of a personal experience or telling a story learned from the pages of a book, storytelling is, by far, the most powerful communications tool of the leader-teacher. Researchers Joanne Martin and Melanie Powers studied the impact that the use of stories has on a speaker's credibility. They found that the use of story provided more credibility than did the statement of a proposition by a trusted leader or the use of empirical data to support a point. People who heard a truth presented in the form of a story were most convinced of both the concept and the credibility of the speaker.[11]

2. ASKING QUESTIONS: Leader-teachers need to learn to ask questions that contribute to learning by challenging thinking. Question-asking is the ability to use questions by design and with intent to generate a challenging and constructive exchange of ideas and insights. To achieve this, questions must be thought provoking. Avoiding questions that can be answered yes and no is a must. Good questions need to engender thought and discussion.

3. CASE STUDIES: Leader-teachers need to learn to use case studies as a way to generate comprehension and application of one's teaching. Creating case studies involves learning the ability to take an experience, actual or simulated, and generate a principled awareness or understanding of the concept being taught. Case studies are complex examples of a concept or problem. They give learners insight into the context of a problem by illustrating the main point being taught. Research documents

that students can learn more effectively when actively involved in the learning process.[12]

4. FIGURES OF SPEECH: Leader-teachers need to be able to use metaphors, objects, proverbs, analogies, illustrations, and other figures of speech to clarify their ideas. The use of figurative language serves to create mental images. The writer or speaker describes something through the use of comparisons to make things clearer. This can be for the purpose of effect, interest, or illustration. The result is a better understanding of the communicator's intended message.

Most often, figurative language is not intended to be interpreted in an absolute sense. Rather, by appealing to the imagination, the use of figurative language provides fresh ways of viewing concepts. Figures of speech make use of a comparison between different things that share a common quality. Figurative language compares two things that are fundamentally different so that their similarities, when pointed out, are seen as interesting, surprising, or distinctive. For example, we often call the Internet the information superhighway. This simple comparison between the invisible world of the Internet and the very visible and easily understood highway system gives the listener a simple means of envisioning the message. That is the power of figurative speech.

Jesus often taught using parables, proverbs, probing questions, and problem-posing. Seldom did He simply just state His point. He often encapsulated His message in a pithy and memorable manner: "Many who are first will be last, and the last first" (Mark 10:31); "You are the salt of the earth. But if the salt loses its saltiness, how can it be made salty again?" (Matthew 5:13); "All who draw the sword will die by the sword" (Matthew 26:52); "For whoever wants to save his life will lose it, but whoever loses his life for me and for the gospel will save it" (Mark 8:35). These are but a few of many examples.

Parables served as analogies through which Jesus could teach complex truths in familiar and concrete terms so that His ideas were understood and accessible to common folk. But His parables did not just illustrate His teachings, they carried His thoughts in a manner that people who were open to hear could hear, and those who were closed to hear could not.

Jesus led by teaching. He did so using common, natural events and circumstances to teach profound concepts. Mustard seeds and fig trees, lost coins and lost sons, wineskins and vineyards all served to communicate His message. For some, His figurative language made His teaching plain. For others, it obscured the truth. It seems from His intentional selection of methods that promote thinking that Jesus must have valued the minds of His learners. He consistently challenged them through His teaching methods.

Great leaders do that. Using the tools of analogy, parable, narrative, and example, they capture the attention of their students and show that they value the abilities of their followers to process concepts.

MODEL THE MESSAGE. Mahatma Gandhi once said, "We must become the change we want to see." James M. Kouzes and Barry Z. Posner researched leaders that people want to follow. They present their findings in their book *The Leadership Challenge*.[13] They discovered that leaders must set an example and build commitment through simple, daily acts that demonstrate the goals they are seeking to achieve. These acts create progress and momentum as followers see that goals are attainable. Kouzes and Posner encourage leaders to model the way through personal example and dedicated execution of the leadership mission. What Kouzes and Posner have verified through research, most effective leaders have known through observation and experience. Leaders who teach most effectively do so by being role models.

In his book *Virtues of Leadership*, William J. Bennett tells the story of a meeting between an old Revolutionary War soldier and the very aged Marquis de Lafayette at a reception for Lafayette in 1824. Lafayette had served with George Washington during the Revolution and was present at the Valley Forge encampment during the dead of the winter of 1777–78. As the old man stood in his uniform, he had a piece of a blanket thrown over his shoulder. He gave Lafayette a salute, which Lafayette immediately returned.

"Do you remember me?" asked the soldier.

"Indeed I cannot say I do," replied Lafayette. The soldier went on to remind the nobleman of the frosty winter at Valley Forge. Lafayette told him that he could not forget those days.

"One bitter night, General Lafayette, you were going the rounds at Valley Forge. You came upon a sentry in thin clothing and without stockings. He was slowly freezing to death. You took his musket, saying, 'Go to my hut. There you will find stockings, a blanket, and a fire. After warming yourself, bring the blanket to me. Meanwhile I will keep guard.'"

The soldier did as told and when he returned to his guard duty, Lafayette took the blanket, cut it in two and handed half to the sentry. That night in 1824, the soldier returned the other half of the blanket to his leader who saved his life and modeled the way.[14]

Lafayette modeled servant-leadership. His act made his leadership easy to take following an act of respect. Leader-teachers must understand the power of modeling. As it has been said, "More is caught than taught." Leader-teachers must grasp that fundamental principle of teaching.

Consider Jesus. He consistently modeled the way for His disciples. In prayer, in conflict, in relationships, and in ministry, He set an example for them to follow.

Jesus clearly taught His disciples to be servant-leaders. In Matthew 20:25–26 He instructed them, "You know that the rulers of the Gentiles lord it over them, and their high officials exercise authority over them. Not so with you. Instead, whoever wants to become great among you must be your servant."

But He does not just tell His disciples to take the role of a servant; He models His teaching. In John 13, Jesus showed humility by doing the task that no one wanted to do. He washed the disciples' feet—a dirty job usually performed by the lowest-ranking person in the room. His disciples were astonished and even uncomfortable.

While they are still trying to understand and process this unexpected and embarrassing event, Jesus states the implications of the action for their lives: "Now that I, your Lord and Teacher, have washed your feet, you also should wash one another's feet. I have set you an example that you should do as I have done for you" (vv. 14–15). It was an act that none of them could ever forget.

What does Jesus require of His disciples? He tells them—us—to do "as" He did. We are to convey His teaching in both word and deed as we practice the selfless love of God through serving one another. If Jesus, who is the Lord, can take the role of servant (*doulos*), then His followers can as well, for a slave is not above his master (v. 16). Leader-teachers must model the actions they expect of others.

The writer of Hebrews grasped this principle of leadership and expressed it with a simple clarity in Hebrews 13:7 where we are encouraged to: "Remember your leaders, who spoke the word of God to you. Consider the outcome of their way of life and imitate their faith."

MINISTER TO PEOPLE. Competent leader-teachers care for and serve those they lead. We have dealt with servant-leadership already, so I will be brief here, but this is a skill each leader-teacher must develop. Ministry to those we lead and teach come through four actions—concern, care, confidence, and consent.

First, a godly leader-teacher must have a true *concern* for those he or she seeks to influence. That concern is expressed in countless ways, but none more powerful than giving of one's time and attention to just listen. Often, I find that just taking a moment with a student or colleague to share a cup of coffee is a ministry in their lives. Over a little "Starbucks brew" one can create a connecting point where real needs are discussed and where you can express your genuine interest in a person. One of the things I enjoy most about my role as a seminary professor is hearing of the joys and struggles of my students. Each day I ask God to renew in me a genuine concern for those I am called to serve, to teach, and to lead, as well as for those who must serve me.

A second way to minister to people is to *care* for them when in need. It is amazing how a relationship can grow out of time spent serving someone who is hurting or who just needs a hand. Paul gained enormous credibility with those he taught because of his care for them. To the Thessalonians he could write,

> As apostles of Christ we could have been a burden to you, but we were gentle among you, like a mother caring for her little children. We loved you so much that we were delighted to share with you not only the gospel of God but our lives as well, because you had become so dear to us. (1 Thessalonians 2:6–8)

There are two classic Christmas stories I enjoy each year. One is *A Christmas Carol* by Charles Dickens, and the other is *It's a Wonderful Life*. Both have a common theme. Two men go through experiences that cause them to examine their lives and the influence they have on others. Through the experience, Dickens's Scrooge is confronted with his lack of care and compassion for his employees. And George Bailey discovers just how important he is in the lives of those he does care for. In both cases, the need for caring leadership is emphasized. Genuine care and compassion for people is basic to a leader's role. In fact, it is at the heart of their effectiveness or ineffectiveness.

A third way to minister to people is to demonstrate your *confidence* in them. Confidence is empowering. Confidence is encouraging. I am convinced that the most debilitating handicap one can have in this world is not physical—it is psychological. It is a lack of self-confidence. No matter how much one might want to achieve, without the confidence that success is possible, people just will not try. Teachers who show confidence in their students open new worlds to them. This is not an unrealistic overstatement of a person's abilities, but a realistic appraisal of the potential in those we seek to lead. One of the things for which I am most grateful to my own mother is the confidence she so freely imparted to me with her often-repeated words, "I know you can do just about anything you set your mind to do." Those words still ring in my memory as her gift to me.

And we must give *consent* to those we lead—that is, believe in their abilities to make decisions and to carry out tasks. We need to allow people room to try and even to fail. Giving consent involves extending trust to others. It means empowering them to act. We minister to those under our charge or our teaching when we support their ideas and dreams. My oldest daughter dreams of working in the broadcasting industry. She is a gifted, attractive, gregarious person who brings excitement into any room she enters. She is capable and energetic. Yes, her dreams are big, but it is my job as a parent to give her consent to pursue those dreams by supporting her even when the challenge is more than just a bit uphill. You see, she needs to know that I know she will succeed.

The Competencies of the Leader

To this point we have looked at four competencies of the teacher. We now turn our attention to the other dimension of the leader-teacher calling—that being leading.

Movies about teams that overcome challenges to become winners always draw me. I love those kinds of stories. In fact, I find them an effective way to teach leadership in my courses at Southern Seminary in Louisville, Kentucky. For example, *Remember the Titans*, the story of the high school football team that had to learn to work together while facing the challenges of racial prejudice and desegregation, teaches the importance of common goals and loyalty. Then there is *Hoosiers*, a movie about a basketball team from a small school in Indiana that wins the state championship. It teaches my students about team unity, the leadership of a coach, and the potential of a group of people fully dedicated to a task. Other films, like *Cool Runnings*, *Miracle*, and *Glory Road* all teach team ministry principles.

But movies about teams need not be sports related. I have used such films as *Ice Age*, *That Thing You Do*, *Flight of the Phoenix*, and *Shrek* to teach the principles of team ministry. The concept of "team" is common in film. That's because teams multiply individual giftedness. Teams are how real change happens. That is why leader-teachers must become competent team coaches. They must learn a few basic skills of coaching if they are to succeed in their leader-teacher calling. We will consider four of these competencies here.

ESTABLISH THE TEAM. The first step in leadership is selecting the team. An essential task of any leader is to select their players. Great coaches know that the selection of the right player is not just about ability; it is also about attitude. The world of professional sports is replete with teams filled with great players that still fail to win. That is because a team is more than able people. Teams are about coordinated, dedicated efforts of individuals who place the team above personal glory. Teams that win are teams that possess a team attitude. In selecting team members, that attitude is indispensable to success.

But ability is important and it cannot be minimized. We need people who are appropriately gifted for the tasks we are asking them to tackle. Some people will be best suited to behind-the-scenes roles while others are out-front people. Giftedness is often a function of one's personality. Effective leaders are able to discern the giftedness of their followers. Jim Collins in *Good to Great* suggests that we not only need the right people on the team, or bus, as he refers to it; we also need them in the right seats on that bus. Team selection is about selecting who is on the bus and then helping those people find where they best fit. It is about both finding the right kind of people, and about helping those people assess the skills that each brings to the team effort.[15]

"Like an archer who wounds at random is he who hires a fool or any passer-by" (Proverbs 26:10). Some people are damaging to a team. Their attitudes or lack of commitment to the effort undermines the leader-teacher. Because they are not part of the team they bring wounds as they shoot their arrows of discontent. When that happens, leaders must understand that team building can mean dropping a player now and then. I once read somewhere that team building is like putting a puzzle together. At times the puzzle box contains extra pieces that belong somewhere else. By forcing a piece into the puzzle, both the piece and the puzzle are damaged. Putting the puzzle together involves carefully selecting team members and carefully placing them in the right place.

EQUIP THE TEAM. A second leadership competency that the teacher-leader must gain is the ability to equip the team. Teams need to be prepared for their task with the right training, a clear game plan, and the best of available equipment—that is the essence of equipping. As a leader-teacher I need to understand that my role includes a responsibility to equip others. Ephesians 4:11–13 is clear about this.

> And He gave some as apostles, and some as prophets, and some as evangelists, and some as pastors and teachers, for the *equipping* of the saints for the work of service, to the building up of the body of Christ; until we all attain to the unity of the faith, and of the knowledge of the Son of God, to a mature man, to the measure of the stature which belongs to the fullness of Christ. (NASB, italics added)

The words "for the equipping of the saints" clearly reveal the function of these leader-teachers. They are to "equip." The New International Version translates this word as "to prepare." It means "to supply with necessities such as tools or provisions." Equipping is what leader-teachers do. They "outfit" God's people for the task of ministry. Biblical leadership involves equipping team members with the training, resources, and assistance needed to use their gifts effectively. God's people are not to "go it alone." They need leader-teachers who will provide the essentials of success. The word *equipping* assumes a team model. Allow me to suggest some basic actions you can take as you seek to equip others for works of service.

1. PROVIDE RESOURCES. These resources may be finances, ministry materials, reading materials, or the equipment necessary to do a task.

2. PROVIDE A REPORTING STRUCTURE. Part of equipping others is requiring accountability and being clear to whom people will be held accountable.

3. SUPPLY ONGOING TRAINING. Training needs to be done on a consistent basis. You cannot just send people to the task of ministry without the training they need to succeed.

4. TAKE TIME TO LISTEN TO YOUR TEAM. It is vital that they know they are valued for who they are and not just what they do. Spend individual time with team members to learn of their needs, concerns, challenges, and joys.

5. PROVIDE OPPORTUNITY FOR YOUR TEAM MEMBERS TO GIVE INPUT AND FEEDBACK. Team members need a time they can communicate with you regarding their role and their experience on the team. Make sure that everyone knows it is okay to ask questions and raise concerns. Ask team members for their input on how you can better equip them for their task. Find out from them what they need to succeed.

6. ESTABLISH EXPECTATIONS. This can be challenging, especially if your team is a group of volunteers. I believe this is best done right from the start and then reviewed from time to time.

Making a team work demands that we focus on one of the most important areas for leadership—the challenges of equipping and enabling a team to achieve its objectives and realize its potential.

EMPOWER THE TEAM. Jesus understood the need to empower His followers. That becomes clear as Jesus commissions His disciples with the task of preaching the gospel. He said to them, "Go into all the world and preach the good news to all creation" (Mark 16:15). This commission is more fully expressed in Matthew's account.

> Then Jesus came to them and said, "All authority in heaven and on earth has been given to me. Therefore go and make disciples of all nations, baptizing them in the name of the Father and of the Son and of the Holy Spirit, and teaching them to obey everything I have commanded you. And surely I am with you always, to the very end of the age." (Matthew 28:18–20)

Biblical leaders must trust those they lead. Paul sensed the responsibility of this empowerment as a stewardship. On several occasions Paul spoke of the gospel "entrusted" to him and others who teach and preach (Romans 3:2; 6:17; 1 Corinthians 4:1; Galatians 2:7; 1 Thessalonians 2:4; 1 Timothy 1:11; 6:20; 2 Timothy 1:12; 1:14; Titus 1:3; 1:7). We ought not take being entrusted lightly. Paul was concerned that he be counted as a trustworthy steward of the gospel. He did not take the Great Commission as simply an interesting suggestion, but as a task for which he would be held accountable.

Empowerment is risky. It means the person who is empowered to act must be the right kind of individual. Paul told Timothy, "The things you have heard me say in the presence of many witnesses *entrust* to reliable men who will also be qualified to teach others" (2 Timothy 2:2, italics added). That word *entrust* describes the concept of empowerment. In order to be effective, at some point a leader must entrust the task to others. To entrust something to someone is to give it to them with the trust that they will handle it with the same care as you would.

Empowerment works that way. Empowerment hands power and authority to another and then trusts them in their use of that power and authority. Before teams can perform at their maximum, they must be empowered for their task. But note the kind of people who are to be empowered or entrusted with leadership. They are to be "reliable" and "qualified." Empowerment follows equipping. Empowerment is biblical, but it is not to be done without great care.

In reaction to hierarchical forms of leadership and as a call to empowerment, Eddie Gibbs writes, "Young leaders are presently demonstrating more egalitarian models of leadership. In today's diverse and rapidly changing world, people on the frontlines must be informed and empowered to make the right decision promptly."[16] Gibbs makes a valid point. He continues, "The church is not alone in its need to develop new models and provide better leadership selection and training."[17] But it is not the times that demand empowerment or trends in contemporary management models; it is the nature of the task. Empowerment has always been God's method of leadership.

If a team is empowered, then it will be more capable of responding to change, and it will be able to focus on the use of its members' giftedness and potential. Empowering a team is a process that can take significant time and effort; but when empowered, team members will derive joy from their work, will be dedicated to the task, will take individual initiative to accomplish tasks, and will support the team process.

ENCOURAGE THE TEAM. Effective leaders understand that all of us need encouragement to perform at our best. The word *encourage* literally means to "give courage to another." How can we give others the courage they need to attempt a challenging task? Encouragement comes from recognizing contributions, valuing individuals, and understanding challenges to success. Learning to encourage others is a skill that can be developed. It can be practiced. Words of encouragement are crucial to successful leadership. "Well done, thou good and faithful servant" is a commendation we all long to hear.

Leader-teachers who only demand and do not encourage are discouragers. They take the joy out of the work and rob followers of a sense of progress. I believe people need to hear that they are doing well far more often than they need to hear correction. I am not talking about false accolades or empty "self-esteem"-building techniques. I am talking about genuine, heartfelt encouragement to every team member.

In their book *Encouraging the Heart*, authors James Kouzes and Barry Posner contend that encouragement "keeps hope alive." They suggest that encouragement of a team involves seven essential actions on the part of leaders. These actions include:

1. Setting clear standards for those we lead
2. Expecting the best of those we lead
3. Paying attention to those who are exemplars of the values and standards
4. Personally recognizing those who serve the team or task well
5. Use stories of team achievement to encourage the team
6. Celebrate team victories together
7. Set an example by doing what you expect of those on the team[18]

Caring for and about people is the most basic quality of the leader-teacher. We have seen that in the previous section when we discussed "ministering to people" as a competency of a teacher. Here we discussed "encouraging the team" as a competency of leadership. Whether in the capacity of teacher or as leader, people are a defining focus of the effective leader-teacher.

At the beginning of this chapter, we told of lack of competence in the Union general Ambrose Burnside. We end now with another Civil War general, Robert E. Lee. With fewer resources and far fewer men, Lee nearly defeated the Union army. Despite the fact that Lee was out-manned, had nowhere near the industrial complex behind his army, had significantly less money, and possessed fewer trained generals, he fought vigorously against the North for four long years. What he had was an army of followers—followers who would do anything for him. Why were they so dedicated to his leadership? Many believe it was his self-less devotion to his troops. One author stated it this way.

If Lee had an example of perfect leadership, it was in the man that he most wanted to follow himself, the God-man of the New Testament. From Him, and from the social tradition of noblesse oblige in which Lee was raised, Lee developed a particular abhorrence of selfishness. . . . he felt "the great duty of life" was "the promotion of the happiness and welfare" of others. As an officer, the great duty was "looking after the men."[19]

Great leaders understand the need to care for and encourage their followers. Lee's dedication to people met that: "Lee's men were willing to go on fighting even though they had outlived their ammunition and food supplies, enduring until death claimed them."[20]

In this chapter we have explored the competencies of the leader-teacher. In the next chapter we will look at one more foundational competency that the leader-teacher must master—that being the skill of leading change. To understand how one leads change, it will be necessary to explore four paradigms of leadership.

Chapter Seven

LEADING CHANGE:
LEADERSHIP PARADIGMS
FOR THE LEADER-TEACHER

"No one pours new wine into old wineskins. If he does, the wine will burst the skins, and both the wine and the wineskins will be ruined. No, he pours the wine into new wineskins."

—Mark 2:22

DICK Fosbury was an American track-and-field athlete who won the gold medal in the high jump event at the 1968 Olympic Games in Mexico City. Using what became known as "the Fosbury flop," Fosbury transformed the sport of high-jumping. He did so by employing a radical new technique. The dominant method of high-jumping was called "the scissors kick" or "straddle." High jumpers would approach the bar facing forward and would swing first one leg and then the other over the bar. But Fosbury struggled to master the standard technique. As strange as it appeared, Fosbury turned his back on the bar and, in the process, forever changed the sport of high jumping. Fosbury threw his body over the bar with his back arched and landed on his shoulders rather than his feet. Jumping 2.24 meters, Fosbury easily took the gold and, in the process, created a new standard technique.

Fosbury was willing to change his methodology to achieve his goal. Like Fosbury, leader-teachers must also be willing to change their approach to the game. Leader-teachers must strategize ways that more effectively accomplish the task at hand given the contexts in which they must lead. In this chapter we will discuss how that change can be practically realized.

Nearly every leader knows the importance of having a clearly defined mission and well-articulated goals. Leaders also understand that if one is to move an organization from the status quo to the attainment of its mission and related goals, an organization or ministry must work through a process marked by change. But how does one enact such change? What is the best way to lead the change process? How that question is answered differs depending on one's philosophy or paradigm of leadership.

Four fundamental paradigms of leadership exist, each driven by a different worldview. These paradigms can be summed up with four simple words—values, vision, venture, and virtues (see figure 7-1). Each of these words identify the distinct perspective that each paradigm brings to our understanding of the process of leading change. Before we consider these paradigms in depth, we will offer a brief summarization.

Figure 7-1
LEADING CHANGE: FOUR PARADIGMS OF LEADERSHIP

Status Quo → VALUES / VISION / VENTURE / VIRTUES → Mission and Goals

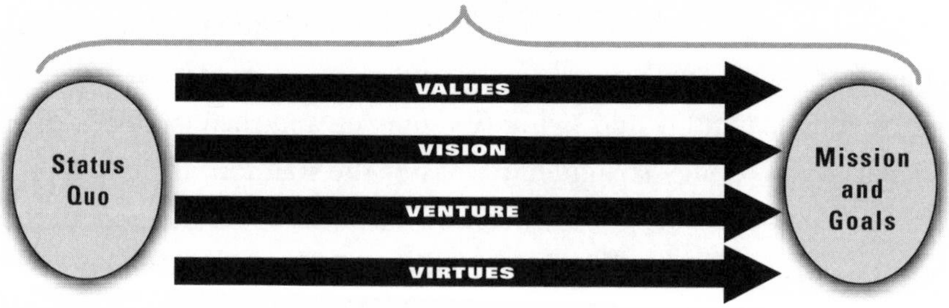

VALUES-DRIVEN LEADERS see change as an action propelled by a team of empowered followers. Leadership begins with a set of values embraced by both leader and follower. These values include a recognition of the worth and dignity of each person. Democratic processes are considered essential with teams functioning as partners working together to achieve goals. Values-driven leaders typically embrace humanistic and existentialistic worldviews, i.e., they place a very high value on people, on intuition, and on shared experience. Leaders are considered stewards of their role and have power only as granted by followers through personal relationships and democratic processes. Leaders are considered servants of the group they lead. Values-driven leaders are coaches and facilitators of a team.

VISION-DRIVEN LEADERS are purpose oriented. They lead by casting motivational goals and by describing a different future where great things occur. They are entrepreneurial and see tomorrow as more productive than today. It is the magnetism and charisma of their personality that compels the entire organization to move forward. Vision-driven leaders are philosophical progressives and typically embrace a pragmatic worldview. They enjoy change and are quite practical in their methods to achieve that change. They see change as inevitable so the goal of the leader is to prepare the organization for that change and capitalize on it.

VENTURE-DRIVEN LEADERS are realists. They know that real change happens as a gradual process through well-devised plans and well-oiled organizational machines. They are good managers who lead through strategizing and structuring. Venture-driven leaders are concerned that change is based on empirical research and data. They seek to establish ventures that will last. They do not act in haste, but rather desire to be careful, analytical, and systematic in their approach. They are managerial leaders. They lead by managing well. Because venture-driven leaders use management practices as their method of leadership, they are often characterized by vision-driven leaders (identified above) as nonleaders.

VIRTUE-DRIVEN LEADERS lead through the strength of their character and the power of their ideas. They are idealists who believe that change should occur with caution as perennial virtues and ideals are upheld and practiced. They are patient leaders. They lead through the proclamation of truth and assume that truth will eventually rule the day.

Leadership is a rational endeavor that involves convincing others of the truth that, if lived faithfully, will bring desired change. They believe that "to think rightly is to behave rightly," so they focus on communicating truth to those who follow. What this means is that they often lead by way of pronouncements. Since they themselves have a high regard for authority, they assume that their followers should as well.

Another way to understand these differing paradigms to leadership is to group them into contemporary and classical approaches. Table 7-1 compares and summarizes these leadership paradigms. In the next section, we will examine them in greater detail.

THE CONTEMPORARY LEADERSHIP PARADIGMS

Two books sit on my desk; both share the same title—*Leading Change*. One is by John P. Kotter,[1] Konosuke Matsushita professor of leadership at Harvard Business School. The other is by James O'Toole,[2] director of the Aspen Institute. Though both were published in the same year, each emphasizes a different aspect of leadership.

Kotter's book is a best seller and probably the most widely implemented theory of change management available today. There is a reason for that—it works. But why wouldn't it? John Kotter is a pragmatist, and his book is a primer on the application of a pragmatic worldview to the field of leadership. In the book, Kotter develops an eight-step approach to leading change. For Kotter, leadership is basically the ability to implement change through visionary leadership, coalition development, and strategic planning processes.

O'Toole's book is not as well-known but has gained numerous endorsements. His work has been endorsed by the likes of Tom Peters,

Table 7-1
FOUR LEADERSHIP PARADIGMS

Contemporary Liberal Empowering Post-Modernity			Classical Conservative Authoritarian Modernity	
Existentialist/humanist	**Pragmatism/progressive**	**Realist**	**Idealist**
Values-driven Communal truth experiential/deconstructed	Vision-driven Relativistic truth situational/constructed	Venture-driven Empirical truth rational/discovered	Virtues-driven Enduring truth absolute/revealed
People are viewed as: good, self-determined, free moral agents	People are viewed as: neutral, interactive with their environment	People are viewed as: neutral, determined by environment	People are viewed as: sinful, determined by fundamental nature
Human relations management theory /Empowerment leadership theory	Contingency/situational leadership theory	Behaviorist leadership theory/ scientific management	Great Man/trait leadership theory
Leadership involves: doing what frees	Leadership involves: doing what works	Leadership involves: doing what's reasonable	Leadership involves: doing what's right
Leader as caregiver and co-laborer	Leader as CEO, visionary leader	Leader as scientific manager	Leader as prophet and scholar
Change occurs by empowerment	Change occurs by development	Change occurs by enactment	Change occurs by pronouncement
Pluralistic church	Pragmatic church	Programmatic church	Proclamation church
Goal: Care for people	Goal: Grow the church	Goal: Advance the work	Goal: Teach the truth
Emerging church movement model	Megachurch movement model	Denominational church model	Reformational church model
Teaching "why"	Teaching "how"	Teaching "for"	Teaching "about"
Teaching should focus on: choices and opportunities	Teaching should focus on: needs and maturational processes	Teaching should focus on: training and rewards	Teaching should focus on: great ideas and thoughts
Narrative teaching methods/Teacher as storyteller	Relevance and needs-based methods/Teacher as change agent	Curriculum-based teaching methods/ Teacher-proof curriculum	Propositional teaching methods/Teacher as authority

author of *In Search of Excellence*; Max De Pree, CEO of Herman Miller, one of the country's largest furniture manufacturers; and Warren Bennis, founding chairman of the Leadership Institute at the University of Southern California's Marshall School of Business and author of more than twenty books on leadership.

O'Toole is existential and humanistic in perspective, and his work is heavily oriented toward *values-driven leadership*. You will recall that values-driven leadership emphasizes the worth and dignity of people. O'Toole rejects the contingency (situational) leadership theory and the pragmatic approaches represented by works like Kotter's. Instead, O'Toole stresses the need for leadership that values people over production processes and product outcomes.

As different as these books appear to be, they do share a common thread—contemporary, postmodern thinking. Kotter follows the direction of the pragmatic wing of postmodernism, while O'Toole follows the existential wing. Both Kotter and O'Toole seek change, based not on the need to achieve some external absolute standard or truth, but based on a belief that change is inevitable and demanded by the constant flow of world events. For Kotter, it is through the implementation of a pragmatic/progressive worldview that such change is best achieved. For O'Toole, change is better realized through the application of a humanistic/existential worldview that values the individual. This promotes self-motivation, which brings changes that the individual recognizes as essential.

EXISTENTIALISTS/HUMANISTS LEADERSHIP THEORY equates leadership with the empowerment of individuals and communities. Existentialist leaders value individual freedom and see the worth and dignity of the individual as the single highest attribute of an excellent organization.

These *values-driven leaders* stress values over vision as the means of bringing about change. To the existentialist/humanistic leader, change results from the exercise of personal freedom, open dialogue, and the experience of genuine community. One cannot force real change on people. It must come from within the person.

As people are valued and as they enter into community relationships, existential leaders believe that people will enact change themselves. Stressing the importance of teams or community, existential leaders see leadership as distributed to all persons.

Values-driven leaders believe that all persons are leaders and that all have a contribution to make in the achievement of group goals. Existentialist/humanistic leaders value people and the personal perspective each individual brings to the team. Existential/humanistic leadership is typically described in leadership literature using terms like *human relations theory, values-based leadership,* or *servant leadership.* Under those headings, existential/humanistic leadership has grown rapidly in the last half of the twentieth century and the early twenty-first century.

PRAGMATISTS/PROGRESSIVE LEADERSHIP THEORY understands leadership as the ability to bring about social and organizational change. Progressives, philosophically speaking, are pragmatic leaders. They emphasize "vision" as the key element in leading change. Leaders are seen as visionaries who perceive a new future as if it were the present. Vision-driven leadership is change-oriented leadership and is situational or contingent in nature.

A prime example of this approach to leadership is the well-known theory of Paul Hersey and Ken Blanchard termed *situational leadership.*[3] For the pragmatic leader, leadership is contingent on a variety of variables that the leader must master. These include the maturity and motivational level of the follower, the situational context, and the personality of the leader. These vision-driven leaders view leadership as an equation in which these variables are in play. Change one variable and the outcome is changed. The task of the pragmatic leader is, therefore, to learn to manipulate and master each variable so that the outcomes of change are achieved.

Here is an important point to note: Both of these approaches to leadership make entirely valid points. In the earlier chapters, I sharply critiqued the postmodern mind-set, both the pragmatic and existential versions, for its lack of commitment to absolutes and for its interpretative approach to truth.

But on these aspects of leading change, postmoderns offer important correctives to the autocratic approach of scientific management that has dominated much of the late nineteenth and early twentieth centuries. Pragmatists are correct in emphasizing the need for visionary leadership. Vision and purpose are certainly critical aspects of effective leadership.

Likewise, existentialists are correct in their emphasis on values and the power of an emancipated follower. Creating empowerment, freedom, and dignity are enormously important aspects of any effective leader's role.

THE CLASSICAL LEADERSHIP PARADIGMS

In contrast to the contemporary leadership paradigms, how does change occur if one leads from the classical realist or idealist perspectives? For both of these approaches, leadership is the shaping—or reforming—of behavior by communication of critical information.

In the case of the *realist*, it is information that is supported by data and the scientific method. For the *idealist*, it is information about unchanging truths and principles that have dominated all cultures through all times. In both cases, the communication of essential information is the paramount task of the effective leader.

REALIST LEADERSHIP THEORY is best known as *scientific management* and can be traced back to the late nineteenth century and early twentieth century. Scientific management is at the heart of venture-driven leadership. It is rooted in industrialization and in the application of the scientific method to the task of production. Leadership, from this viewpoint, is the efficient management of any venture so as to accomplish a task with the greatest possible level of effectiveness.

Through the use of research, scientific analysis, and careful management practices, programs are designed to achieve desired ends. These programs are fine-tuned until the best possible means of accomplishing the task are determined and implemented. Once achieved, change only occurs when overwhelming evidence demonstrates that the program is no longer achieving the intended purpose.

Venture-driven leaders are typically slower to change than are values-driven or vision-driven leaders, but they will change when the data demands it. Once a program is established, venture-driven leaders will proclaim, "If it ain't broke, don't fix it."

In the remake of the film *Cheaper by the Dozen*, Steve Martin plays a college coach with twelve children. The family moves from their small-town world to a major city and the father to the role of a Big Ten football coach. It was a humorous movie that had a solid draw at the box office. But beyond the title and a common number of offspring, this film had little in common with the 1950 film.

The first version of *Cheaper by the Dozen* was based on the book by Frank B. Gilbreth Jr. and Ernestine Gilbreth Carey. It is a true story written from the perspective of the Gilbreth children as they grew up with their father, Frank Gilbreth, a turn-of-the-century "efficiency expert." Frank Gilbreth obsessively and fanatically applied scientific management principles to running his household. In the film, Gilbreth is seen using a stopwatch to time every family task as he searched for ways to improve efficiency. His efforts included timing his children as they greeted him when he returned from a business trip and counting every movement his wife made in doing the laundry with the hope of making her work more efficient. The film provides an interesting look at scientific management applied in the extreme.

Scientific management theory has undergone countless revisions since it was detailed by Frederick Winston Taylor (1856–1917) in his book *The Principles of Scientific Management*.[4] Taylor believed that every task could be understood scientifically, ordered systematically, and eventually mechanized. He believed the result would be increased quantity and quality of production. The leader's role, from Taylor's point of view, is to set production goals, discover critical information to improve the production process, design programs to achieve goals, and manage laborers in the task.

Others, like Henri Fayol (1841–1925), established the foundational principles of scientific management. In his book *General and Industrial Management*,[5] Fayol puts forth fourteen principles of management that have become the primary doctrines of scientific management theory. Its authority was so powerful in Western society that the principles of scientific management theory have influenced almost everyone serving in an executive role to this day in that his work is foundational to nearly every textbook on management practice.

IDEALIST LEADERSHIP THEORY is most commonly called the *Great Man Theory of Leadership*. Its roots go back to Aristotle, who believed that social rank is determined through the superiority of one's virtues— knowledge, wisdom, competence, talent, and ability. For Aristotle, such virtues are, by nature, a circumstance of birth. Thus, leaders are born, not made.[6]

Coach Bobby Knight once spoke to an Indiana University School of Business class in leadership. Knight took the podium and began his lecture: "The first thing you people need to know about leadership," he told the students, "is that most of you simply don't have it in you." Knight was without a doubt a Great Man theorist when it came to his view of leadership. To Knight, leadership is something inherent in a person from birth and is not something that can be taught. This is a common view of the idealist. Virtues-driven leadership grows out of qualities of the person, many of which are inborn.

The Great Man theory held sway until the late nineteenth and early twentieth centuries. Until social science research challenged the notion, it was commonly held that leaders possessed that elusive quality: leadership. The consensus was that leaders differed from followers in fundamental qualities such as intelligence, the moral force of one's character, personal charisma, and energy level. These traits were not learned, though they may be developed through education, but were instead determined by fate, the course of history, and divine providence.

This viewpoint meant that leaders were seen as especially gifted to influence the lives of others. Current proponents of this theory point to persons such as Thomas Jefferson, Benjamin Franklin, Abraham Lincoln, Martin Luther, John Kennedy, and Martin Luther King Jr. as examples of great men whose intrinsic abilities matched the situational events of their times. Thus, this view sees leadership as the right, privilege, and duty of the superior few.

In the last sixty years, the Great Man theory has taken a backseat to behavioral and situational theories of leadership. The social sciences have prompted extensive research into the matter of leadership, producing data that both challenges and confirms aspects of the Great Man theory.

Warren Bennis and Burt Nanus reject the Great Man theory. They vehemently challenge the belief that leaders are born and not made. Leadership, they believe, is a learned skill and has little to do with innate traits.

> Biographies of great leaders sometimes read as if they had entered the world with an extraordinary genetic endowment, that somehow their future leadership role was preordained. Don't believe it. The truth is that major capacities and competencies of leadership can be learned, and we are all educable, at least if the basic desire to learn is there and we do not suffer from learning disorders. Furthermore, whatever natural endowments we bring to the role of leadership, they can be enhanced; nurture is far more important than nature in determining who becomes a successful leader.[7]

However, researchers Shelley A. Kirkpatrick and Edwin A. Locke would disagree with Bennis and Nanus. Their research supports the contention that some people are better suited to leadership than others and that leadership does arise out of some fundamental virtues of the individual. They write:

Regardless of whether leaders are born or made . . . it is unequivo-
cally clear that leaders are not like other people. Leaders do not have to
be great men or women by being intellectual geniuses or omniscient
prophets to succeed, but they do need to have the "right stuff" and this
stuff is not equally present in all people. Leadership is a demanding,
unrelenting job with enormous pressures and grave responsibilities. It
would be a profound disservice to leaders to suggest that they are ordi-
nary people who happened to be in the right place at the right time. . . .
In the realm of leadership (and in every other realm), the individual
does matter.[8]

The "right stuff"—that is the essense of the idealistic approach to
leadership. Leadership is about leaders who possess virtues that make
them distinct from others. Identify those virtues, and you can select leaders. Teach those virtues, and you can develop leaders.

THE REST OF THE STORY

So what is the answer? Should leadership be values-driven, vision-
driven, venture-drives, or virtues-driven? A complete theory of leadership must answer: all of the above. From a biblical perspective,
leadership involes each of these dimensions.

Biblical leaders value people as divine image-bearers. They are
hope-filled and visionary because they know God continues to do great
things in this world. They are venturous as they establish churches,
Christian organizations, mission efforts, new programs, and efforts to
meet human needs. And they are virtuous leaders who seek to do all of
their ministry in a manner consistent with the character of Christ and
the principles of God's Word.

Leader-teachers bring change through a combination of values, vision, venture, and virtues. But that does not tell the whole story. As
leader-teachers, biblical leaders understand their role as a calling to both
lead and teach. They lead through various means—but it is teaching that

is primary. To bring individual life change, organizational change, and societal change, they understand that some very basic competencies must be practiced.

In the previous chapter we discussed these competencies. We said they serve as fence posts giving stability and strength to our leadership. The slats in our fence are values, vision, venture, and virtues. When constructed together, real change—biblical change and enduring and godly change—is possible. Figure 7-2 reveals the relationship between the competencies of a leader-teacher and the four leadership paradigms discussed in this chapter.

Figure 7-2
LEADING BY TEACHING: THE PROCESS OF CHANGE

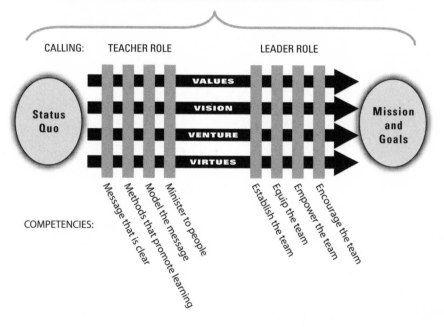

Change then occurs not as a simple pragmatic steplike process or because we empower people. Likewise, leading change is not an orchestrated management process or the result of an authoritative proclamation from an authority figure. Change is the result of a dynamic process that includes elements of all of these.

One thing is for certain—change is inevitable and learning to adapt is a fundamental skill of a leader-teacher. Leading change calls for a willingness to revise methods, change techniques, and strive forward. Leadership will require a willingness to retain a commitment to foundational matters as the classical leadership models require while adjusting to the culture as contemporary models of leadership promote.

Chapter Eight

LEADERSHIP IN CONTEXT:
FOUR BASIC TYPES OF CHURCHES

*Yet a time is coming and has now come when the true wor-
shipers will worship the Father in spirit and truth, for they
are the kind of worshipers the Father seeks. God is spirit, and
his worshipers must worship in spirit and in truth.*

—John 4:23–24

*Even so faith, if it has no works, is dead, being by itself. But
someone may well say, "You have faith and I have works;
show me your faith without the works, and I will show you
my faith by my works."*

—James 2:17–18 (NASB)

ON Monday, August 29, 2005, Hurricane Katrina struck the city of
New Orleans along with the rest of the Louisiana and Mississippi Gulf
Coast. Katrina unleashed an amount of energy greater than two hundred times the electrical generating capacity of all of Earth's power
plants combined.[1] The result was a catastrophe involving broken levees, walls of water, and billons of dollars worth of property damage.
There were over eleven hundred deaths in Louisiana and the entire Gulf
Coast region. For days after the hurricane, the blame game was under
way. The news media blasted city, state, and federal leaders for failing

to prepare and meet the needs of those who fell victim to this disaster. Leaders at all levels blamed one another. But what was lost in the coverage and the conflict was the context of the event itself.

For nearly three hundred years, New Orleans existed below sea level. Surrounded on three sides by water and with levees designed to withstand a Category Three hurricane, New Orleans was a disaster waiting for its moment in history. As a matter of record, the news coverage for several days leading up to the flood described, in detail, the potential events that would be experienced if a worst-case scenario materialized. One CNN news reporter, John Zarrella, explained those potential events in a hauntingly accurate report aired several hours before the disaster actually occurred. But it wasn't long after the predictions became reality that the historic and geographic context of the unfolding situation was forgotten.

Live video feeds from various locations around New Orleans had the effect of ripping individual stories out of the larger context. As a result, people almost immediately became angry at what they believed to be federal leadership failure and a delayed governmental response. Some raised issues of racism, while others identified incompetence as the reason for a delay in getting people much-needed food and water.

But if taken in the true context of the circumstances and the region's history, it seems that at least some of that initial anger may have been misplaced. While what occurred had indeed been predicted, most of the events of that day in August were not under human control. The circumstances that unfolded did so because this catastrophe destroyed infrastructures and systems that were designed for normal, day-to-day life. Over time, growing knowledge of the sheer magnitude of this calamity provided the context needed to make a valid judgment of leader or rescuer performance. Again, if context is taken into account, one is more inclined to judge the situation and what followed with greater empathy for those in leadership positions at all levels.

Context is essential. Whether one is interpreting world events, the meaning of a statement made in a personal conversation, or the interpretation of biblical passage, context plays a defining role. To lift words or events out of their context is to strip those words or events of their meaning.

Imagine, for example, pulling a single line item from a church financial report and then trying to understand it without reference to the context in which the money was spent. Is $6,000 a little or a lot of money? If it is the total cost of shingling the church's leaky roof, it may well be considered to be quite a reasonable amount and a church would probably be quite happy with that low number in a budget. But if the youth group raised $6,000 toward hurricane disaster relief, this amount is likely to be considered a lot of money, worthy of encouragement and praise. You see, context is important to understanding almost any idea or event. Similarly, context is fundamental when it comes to leadership.

Christian leadership demands that we are able to understand the context of our ministry. In my years of serving in pastoral ministry, doing church consultation, and teaching in both the Bible college and seminary setting, I have observed a disturbing fact. While many pastoral leaders are able to skillfully exegete the literary, historical, and cultural context of a Scripture passage, they are equally unskilled in their ability to critically analyze the context of their church ministry environment. This lack of skill results in the limited ability of leader-teachers to have the impact they desire.

In this chapter we will examine four different types of church ministry contexts. Because these models grow out of broader philosophical perspectives, many of the concepts we discuss will apply beyond the church as well.

ASSESSING THE SPIRITUAL STYLE OF YOUR CHURCH

Churches have their own personality, or what I like to call *spiritual style*. Enter a Southern Baptist Church in Alabama, an Evangelical Free Church in Minnesota, or a Lutheran Church in New York State and you will discover not only denominational distinctives, but also clear differences in how worship and overall ministry is conducted. While many of these worship and ministry characteristics are rooted in theology, others have an historical or cultural derivation. Still others reflect the uniqueness of the church itself and its lineage of formal leadership. Whatever the cause, these differences affect the way a church is led, especially if one seeks to lead through teaching.

Denominational and theological differences are fairly easy to detect. Many of these can be found in the creedal, covenantal, and even legal documents of the church. There are certain practices that are essentially Baptist in nature and others that reflect a Methodist or Brethren understanding of the church and its nature.

But other differences may be more difficult for the leader to discern. Even within the same denomination, church cultures can diverge widely from one another in terms of their spiritual style. Leader-teachers, both laymen and paid pastoral staff, would benefit by studying the spiritual style and culture of the church that they are called to lead. This knowledge helps the leader-teacher to place the work into a context so that they can better interpret experiences, church communication, conflict, and the change process. By understanding a church's spiritual style, the leader-teacher can at first match their leadership style to the church and then, over time, guide the church in innovative directions. Additionally, leaders can compare their gift-mix to the spiritual style of the church in order to determine if there is a good fit and potential for effective service. Assuming that this knowledge is beneficial to both the leader and to the church, how then does one go about this assessment process?

Over the years I have met with a number of churches in an effort to help them gain direction, improve leadership effectiveness, and move the church forward. When I consult with churches, my assessment process begins with a study of two key biblical passages. The first is John 4:23–24. The second is James 2:14–26. Let's consider these two passages briefly.

Spirit and Truth: John 4:23–24

The roads of Samaria were hot and dusty. Needing a drink of cool water, Jesus stopped at Jacob's well outside the Samaritan village of Sychar. At that well, Jesus met a woman who was also there to draw water. To her surprise, Jesus paused for a moment in His travels and engaged her in a conversation. Now it is important to remember that historically and traditionally, Jewish men, much less a rabbi, did not speak in public to women, even their own wives.

But Jesus did not define His ministry by historical or traditional standards. He spoke to her, not because she was a woman of affluence or influence, for such women did not draw water from wells in those times, and not because He simply wanted to break with tradition. He knew her life was disrespectable, yet Jesus still valued her.

What ensued was a discussion of her life situation and spiritual needs. In the context of that conversation, Jesus made a plain statement about true worship. He said, "A time is coming and has now come when the true worshipers will worship the Father in spirit and truth, for they are the kind of worshipers the Father seeks. God is spirit, and his worshipers must worship in spirit and in truth" (John 4:23–24). "Spirit and in truth"—those two dimensions of worship help us to identify one aspect of a church's spiritual style.

It is important to note that Jesus did not emphasize one aspect of genuine worship over the other. We are to worship in both spirit and truth. In practice, however, churches tend to exhibit one quality more than the other. Churches tend to be either more "spirit-oriented" or "truth-oriented" in their spiritual or worship style.

The concept of spirit and truth orientations is not new. In fact, Bernard Ramm told us that "the great motto of the Reformation in the sixteenth century was 'the Word and the Spirit.'"[2] Mary Stewart Van Leeuwen further explained this distinction.

In the narrowest sense, Word meant the revealed and inspired Holy Scripture; and correspondingly, the Spirit meant the Holy Spirit. Both terms, however suggest clusters of ideas. "Word" suggests the truth claims of Christianity, the meaning of the texts of Scripture, and the formulation of the contents of Scripture into theology. . . . The "Word" concept encapsulates the rational, articulated, objective aspect of the redeemed Christian life, whose lynchpin is the unchanging standard of Scripture and its rationally evolved theologies. On the other hand, Spirit . . . encompasses that aspect of the redeemed Christian life, which is richly experiential, emotional, personal and interpersonal, embracing the supernatural quality of our ongoing dialogue with God and with our brothers and sisters in Christ.[3]

In a follow-up article, Ramm explains the importance of a balance between spirit and truth (Word as he refers to it). He states,

A healthy, normative and powerful Christianity is the proper balance and relationship of Word and Spirit. However, the history of the church reveals different periods when this balance was lost. Either too much was said of the Word at the expense of the Spirit, or too much of the Spirit at the expense of the Word. At times of intense doctrinal conflict, there is always the temptation to become so precise in our theology that we forget that the truth of Scripture needs the reinforcement and enlightenment of the Spirit of truth. When such a high premium is placed on correct theology, there is the further temptation to define a Christian as the one who believes the right theology—a kind of theological intellectualism of sorts . . . at times of spiritual lethargy or powerlessness, or too much ecclesiastical "overhead," some sort of movement of the Spirit sets in. It is a protest against "dead orthodoxy" or "lifeless liturgy" or powerless preaching or lack of a rich devotional life. Pietism arose in orthodox Lutheran Germany to protest the deadness of such an intensely theological understanding of Christianity. Methodism arose in England when the Anglican church was in need of such reform but seemed powerless to bring it to pass. Pentecostalism emerged in the nineteenth century when Christianity was becoming more and more defined by denominationalism and when there were serious inroads of rationalism in the Christian church. "[4]

Table 8-1 identifies the characteristics of churches in these basic categories. For now, take a look at the table and see if you can picture a church that reflects the kind of descriptors listed. Following the table is an explanation of spirit-oriented and truth-oriented churches.

Table 8-1
SPIRIT AND TRUTH ORIENTATION

SPIRIT

- Intuition
- Encounter with God
- Paradigm shifts
- Relevance
- Mystical
- Spiritual formation

- Authentic experience
- Subjective
- Cultural accommodation
- Immanence of God
- Expressive
- Community of believers

John 4:23–24

- Information
- Theology of God
- Unchanging ideals
- Biblical
- Empirical
- Christian education

- Authority
- Objective
- Supracultural absolutes
- Transcendence of God
- Structured
- Commitment of the believer

TRUTH

WHAT ARE THE MARKS OF A SPIRIT-ORIENTED CHURCH? Enter a spirit-oriented church and you will discover an emphasis on the intuitive side of the Christian faith and on the promotion of a very personal encounter with the living God. God is understood to be immanent (close), meaning that God desires a very intimate and even mystical relationship with the individual believer.

Relationships between believers are also highly valued, the importance of which shows in the prominent teachings on Christian community, the family of God, and on "body life." These teachings are often but not always accompanied by a theological openness to the sign gifts (prophecy, tongues, etc.) and other more subjective means of hearing the voice of God. Spirit-oriented churches tend to attract those seeking a far more expressive Christian worship experience.

Change is valued in the spirit-oriented churches because of the heartfelt desire to remain "in step" with the work of the Holy Spirit. It is often believed that change proves God's Spirit is at work. Even when teaching from the Bible is the focus in a spirit-oriented church, *relevant* teaching and preaching is emphasized because of the desire to be culturally connected. Evangelistically, spirit-oriented churches attract individuals who seek a more mystical and "authentic" experience with the God of the Bible.

Spirit-oriented churches tend to use terms like "spiritual formation" to describe individual spiritual growth. Spirit-oriented Christians are convinced that spiritual formation is a community process occurring most effectively when all believers openly and authentically live their faith, problems and all, within the context of a church family. As Ramm made clear in the quote above, spirit-oriented churches often develop as a reaction to "dead orthodoxy" and "lifeless liturgy," i.e., an excessive emphasis on theological reflection as the essence of Christianity, more than experience.

WHAT ARE THE MARKS OF A TRUTH-ORIENTED CHURCH? If you walked into a truth-oriented church this Sunday, you would probably note some very clear indicators of this commitment. First, you would observe the prominent place of preaching and teaching of the Scriptures through the worship and educational ministry of the church. Truth-oriented churches believe wholeheartedly in the power of the Word of God to change lives. Change comes by hearing and hearing by the Word of God. Therefore, truth-oriented churches make the proclamation of truth their highest priority. Truth-oriented churches are careful about matters of theology, especially their theology of God. With an enormous respect for God as almighty and transcendent (that is, distinctively other than His creation), truth-oriented churches have a tendency to focus on information about God and minimize an emphasis on a more mystical, personal encounter with God.

Truth-oriented churches value absolutes. This commitment to absolute truth brings great stability to these churches. With that stability comes structure, tradition, and a desire to remain doctrinally faithful. Rejecting the intuitive and subjective tendencies of the spirit-oriented churches, truth-oriented churches look to objective truth and empirical findings for reliable direction. Christian education in the truth-oriented congregation is scholastic in design and often uses a lecture approach to teaching and discipleship. Communicating content in this way is preferred to the more "fuzzy-minded" spiritual formation processes of the spirit-oriented church.

Given Jesus' emphasis on the need for both spirit and truth in our worship practice, it is probably best not to think of these qualities as pure dichotomy. It is better to think of the spirit-truth distinction as a continuum. The fact is that most churches are somewhere on a continuum between spirit and truth, with one emphasis dominating the other. The leader-teacher must learn to diagnose where on this continuum their church would be located.

Where do you believe your church falls on this continuum? In order to help you better diagnose your church's spiritual style, I have included an inventory at the end of this chapter that I use with church board members when we meet together. It is certainly not complex, but it does allow church leaders a means of self-evaluation.

YOUR CHURCH?   YOUR CHURCH?

Spirit ------ |------ |---X--|------ ·|-----·|---X---| -----|----- Truth
Oriented   Oriented

Faith and Works: James 2:14–26

A second passage that I explore with church leaders when I do consultations is James 2:14–26. This passage presents the interdependent relationship of faith and works in the life of the believer and the local church.

Scripture is abundantly clear that works and faith go hand-in-hand. We are certainly not saved by our works, we are saved by faith and faith alone. Paul states this essential truth emphatically when he teaches about the "righteousness that comes by faith" (Romans 4:13). But Scripture is equally clear that "faith without deeds is dead" (James 2:26). "I will show you my faith by what I do," James says (2:18). John Calvin summarized this well: "Faith alone justifies, but the faith which justifies is not alone."

Those who are true followers of Christ will possess both faith and works. Again, like spirit and truth, it is not an either/or proposition. Both are essential in the life of a follower of Jesus. But in reality, most of our ministries tend to emphasize one to a greater measure than the other. I find that some churches are more easily identified as "works-oriented churches" while other are more "faith-oriented churches." Now, I am not referring to their theology of salvation, but to their practice of ministry. Table 8-2 provides a summary of my observations as I consult with church leaders.

Table 8-2
FAITH- AND WORKS-ORIENTED CHURCHES

JAMES 2:14–26	
Works	Faith
• Task-oriented	• Reflection-oriented
• Action directed	• Process directed
• Doing	• Contemplation
• Purpose-driven	• Relationships
• Externally focused	• Internally focused
• Church growth = Numbers/size	• Church growth = Health/maturity
• Programming	• Personalization
• Organization emphasis	• Organism emphasis
• Church as an enterprise	• Church as a family

WHAT ARE THE MARKS OF A WORKS-ORIENTED CHURCH? Works-oriented churches are busy places. They tend to be driven by the tasks of ministry. They take the Great Commission quite seriously as they create programs to carry it out. They have a low tolerance for words without accompanying action. Leaders in these churches are often "type A" personalities who think of themselves as the church's CEO. Works-oriented churches often model themselves after the church of Acts 2, viewing the last six verses of that chapter as purpose statements for the church. Books like *The Purpose-Driven Church* are foundational reading for the works-oriented leader. Leaders in these churches tend to see church ministry as an "enterprise."[5] As a Christian enterprise, many of these churches offer highly developed programs for all age levels as they seek to aggressively affect their community for Christ.

Works-oriented churches gauge growth and progress in terms of numbers. Like a business, growth is seen as quantifiable and measurable. Works-oriented churches typically have strong organizational structures led by gifted professionals. In most works-oriented churches, public ministry occurs with a high degree of excellence because works-oriented churches want things done right. A commitment to excellence and achievement is part of the DNA of these churches. That being the case, the works-oriented church is far more likely to hire professional staff to lead various ministry areas that they feel cannot be left to unprepared or unprofessional volunteers.

WHAT ARE THE MARKS OF A FAITH-ORIENTED CHURCH? Faith-oriented churches are quite different from the works-oriented church. First, they are far more reflective and theological in their approach to ministry. They desire a deep understanding of the faith. Less focus is placed on programs and more on individual personal relationships. Though not always the case, these churches tend to be small in size and feel homey and family-like when you visit them.

Because they are focused on authentic faith experience, faith-oriented churches provide more opportunities for average individuals to minister publicly. They tend to be less concerned about the professionalism of public ministry and are focused on helping people contemplate issues regarding their personal faith walk through the use of their gifts and talents. To their detriment, many of the faith-oriented churches I have worked with over the years are internally focused, i.e., they are not nearly as evangelistically-oriented or as seeker-sensitive as most works-oriented churches are. They believe that evangelism is done by the individual apart from the church setting and that the purpose of church is to worship and contemplate God.

To their credit, faith-oriented churches tend to define church growth in terms of quality rather than quantity. They measure growth in terms of spiritual nurture and the maturation of each individual within the congregation through participation in the community of believers. Rather than describing the church as an organization, they much prefer to see it as a living organism. As with the works-oriented church, they too look to Acts 2:41–47 as verses that define the church. But faith-oriented churches emphasize the *koinonia* (fellowship) aspects of the passage. They stress the fact that a spirit-led church is a church that meets the needs of its people on a personal level.

Leaders in faith-oriented churches tend to be reflective individuals. I have found these leaders to be of two basic types. One is very personable, caring, and highly pastoral. This leader listens well and is strong at providing for the ministry needs of individuals. He tends to be introspective and contemplative when it comes to matters of faith. Out of these introspections comes a deep desire to love people and minister to their needs.

The second type of leader is equally pensive, but is far less people-oriented. This leader reflects on theological matters and focuses on the character and nature of God. He desires to bring a sense of divine awe to his followers as he helps them understand the God they worship.

As with the spirit-truth distinction, it is best not to think of these qualities as strict dichotomy. It is wiser to view works and faith on a continuum. Again, all churches have characteristics of both the works and faith orientations, for this is not an either/or proposition. However, in my experience, churches do tend toward one end of the continuum more than the other. When I meet with leaders, I often ask them to consider where they would locate their church on the work-faith continuum on the next page. It is always interesting to me to see just how much agreement can be found among a group of church leaders with regard to their church context. The leader-teacher must learn to diagnose where the church they are serving would be located on the work-faith continuum if they are to lead in a way consistent with the context. So where do you believe your church falls on this continuum? Again, in order to aid you as you diagnose your church's spiritual style, I have included an inventory at the end of this chapter.

YOUR CHURCH?   YOUR CHURCH?

Faith ------ |------ |---X--|------·|-----·|---X---| -----·|----Works
Oriented   Oriented

FOUR TYPES OF CHURCHES

To this point we have been trying to understand the contexts in which leadership must occur. We have been focused on two continuums, the spirit-truth continuum and the works-faith continuum. By bringing these two dimensions of spiritual style together in a single model, it is now possible to identify four distinctive types of churches. Again, while no church ministry fits completely in one quadrant (remember, these are continuums and not dichotomies), most churches locate predominately within a particular spiritual style. For those who react negatively to these models as "pigeonholing," keep in mind that this is intended to be descriptive information, not a prescriptive requirement. Also, remember that if you do find that your church fits one of these quadrants you have discovered this from a self-reporting instrument. In other words, it is your own observations that placed your church in one of the quadrants, we will be studying. The goal here is to help you identify the context in which you are called to lead and then to match your style to the leadership needs of that context. Also, this exercise is not designed to be a critique of any particular ministry or church. Take a close look at table 8–3 on the next page. Compare it with table 7–1 in the previous chapter. You will probably see some interesting connections between a church's paradigm of leadership and spiritual style of ministry.

Four types of churches emerge for us from our considerations of the spirit-truth and works-faith continuums.

- THE PROCLAMATION CHURCH—This church is truth-oriented and faith-oriented in its characteristics.

- THE PROGRAM CHURCH—This church is truth-oriented and works-oriented in its characteristics.
- THE POWER CHURCH—This church is spirit-oriented and works-oriented in its characteristics.
- THE PLURALISTIC CHURCH—This church is spirit-oriented and faith-oriented in its characteristics.

Table 8-3
FOUR TYPES OF CHURCHES

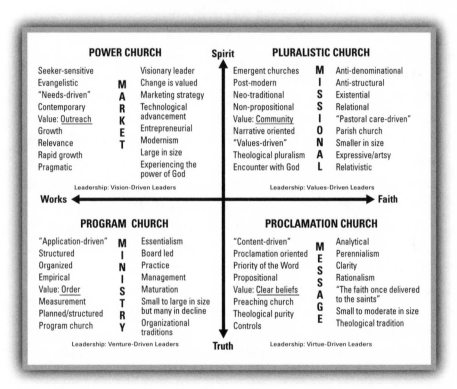

The Proclamation Church

As I entered the church it was obvious what was valued here. Each person was carrying a Bible, the pulpit was massive and conspicuously located in the center of the platform, and the bulletin contained an outline of the sermon. It took only minutes to sense that biblical preaching and teaching were the dominant purpose of the morning services.

Before the service at which I was to speak, I attended the adult Sunday school class. Adults met for Bible study in a classroom format where most of the teaching was conducted in a lecture style. Seats were arranged in rows with minimal opportunity for student interaction. The teacher was at the front, behind a lectern. When the class began, a few minutes were taken for the sharing of prayer requests, but it was clear that the teacher's lesson was the purpose of this adult Sunday school session.

The service that followed was rather formal with three or four hymns, a Scripture reading, special music performed by a soloist, a choir number, and the offering being the primary components—that is, until the sermon. I was told in advance that the message given was to be no less than forty minutes in length and was to be highly analytical and expository in its content, structure, and style.

Proclamation churches are heavily driven by biblical content. Priority is given to the preaching and teaching of God's Word with the goal being the transformation of listeners who hear and act on its propositional truth. Consistently embracing theological orthodoxy, proclamation churches value clear belief and doctrinal purity. Great concern exists with regard as to who does the teaching and what is taught. Therefore, these churches require significant control over the teaching ministry of the pulpit and the classroom podium by the church leaders. In many cases, these churches are marked by a strong theological history and tradition that is venerated.

These are truth-oriented and faith-oriented churches. While spirit-oriented churches emphasize reflection on one's personal spiritual encounter with God, faith- and truth-oriented proclamation churches invest far more energy into reflecting on "the faith that was once for all entrusted to the saints" (Jude 1:3). Thus, preachers are expected to be biblical scholars, and preaching serves as the vehicle for the communication of that scholarship.

The proclamation church is led by such pastors as John MacArthur (pastor of Grace Community Church in Sun Valley, California), John Piper (pastor of Bethlehem Baptist Church in Minneapolis), and D. James Kennedy (pastor of Coral Ridge Presbyterian Church in Fort Lauderdale, Florida). Its theologians and spokespersons include Millard J. Erikson (Professor of Theology at Western Seminary in Portland, Oregon), Donald A. Carson (Professor of New Testament at Trinity Evangelical Divinity School in Deerfield, Illinois), R.C. Sproul (Professor of Theology and Apologetics at Knox Theological Seminary in Fort Lauderdale, Florida), Wayne Grudem (Professor of Theology and Bible at Phoenix Seminary) and numerous others.

The strengths and weaknesses of the proclamation church are important to note. Proclamation churches are strong in their unwavering commitment to the truth of God's Word and to historic orthodox theology. They place a high value on truth, and pastors preach that truth with genuine conviction. Their preaching is exegetically solid and expository in format. Their leaders are driven by biblical virtues, believing that leaders should personally model those virtues.

On the negative side, the leadership in these churches is at times perceived as authoritarian, exclusionary, and graceless. This perception has prompted reactions from other evangelicals who complain that proclamation church leaders are rigid and narrow.[6] Proclamation church leaders would do well to be reminded from these criticisms that their confident communication can be misunderstood. Because their words carry so much weight, they must be cautious that their communication does not project a sense of condescension or elitism. If they fail to take intentional measures to show otherwise, proclamation churches can be perceived as cold and uncaring about relational issues.

Though some of these churches are large, most are not. Those that are large in size are often built on the reputations of their preacher. But again, most are much smaller ministries. Leaders of proclamation churches must cultivate other aspects of ministry besides preaching, such as pastoral care, evangelistic outreach, and personal relationships. Unless balance is present, these churches, when taken to an extreme, can be so separated from the culture as to become irrelevant and marginal in their impact. If leaders in these churches are not wise, they can slide into a "Christ against culture" approach and mentality that will leave them marginalized and only preaching to the choir.[7]

Faithful to the message, the proclamation church produces highly informed and biblically literate parishioners. Linked to a Christian version of idealistic philosophy, proclamation churches present a perennial message that attendees can trust.

The Program Church

The program church is everywhere. It is aging, but it still thrives in many places. The program church is dedicated to practicing the truth in practical ways. Program churches can be any size, but most have been around awhile and many are in decline. Program churches are highly organized, committee structured, usually board-led, and traditional in their mode of operation.

Some great ministries fit the program model. Moody Memorial in Chicago, First Baptist Church in Dallas, Wheaton Bible Church, and Brandywine Valley Baptist Church in Wilmington, Delaware, are just a few examples of churches that thrive using the programming approach. Combining an unwavering commitment to Scripture, a strong pulpit ministry, and a mature group of highly committed leaders, these churches have a proven ability to manage effective programs that make a difference in individual lives, in families, and in their communities.

However, many churches in the program model were started between fifty and a hundred years ago by visionary leaders, but have, over time, become ingrown and ineffective in reaching unchurched people. In many cases, program churches once enjoyed significant growth and thriving ministries. They retain solid doctrine, hierarchical systems of polity, and mature organizational structures. Many were part of the Bible church movement of the fifties, sixties, and seventies. As mainline denominational churches strayed from the belief that the Bible is the inerrant Word of God, a Bible-teaching vacuum was created. Independent, newly planted churches—"Bible Churches"—grew to fill that vacuum. These churches shared a common commitment to the central place of the Bible in the life of the church, embracing its authority and holding that salvation is found by grace through faith in Christ alone.

It has been my experience in meeting with church leaders to discover that program churches are often flagship churches in their respective denominations and that they still maintain strong denominational ties. Program church pastors I have met are concerned about their aging congregations, dated facilities, and the downward trends their churches are experiencing in attendance.

Many of these churches find themselves islands in seas of change. Around them, neighborhoods have demographically shifted—a change not well reflected in the congregation. For board members in these churches, leadership has become the management of past gains and their prevailing task is ministry maintenance. They are rarely energized by the establishment of new ministry endeavors. In fact, fearing new directions, change is many times resisted by leaders in these churches.

But it is not all bad news or hopeless in the program church. Program churches have strengths on which they can capitalize. They typically have some dedicated members and leaders who have learned to give generously. Many people are mature believers who truly love Christ and, if challenged appropriately, are willing to take needed corrective actions to restart the church.

These are churches dedicated to acting on their faith. What is needed is leadership that helps them grasp their situation empirically and can challenge them to become a turnaround church. When that happens, they can become fresh and lively ministries that have an almost instant impact in the community. You see, they are good at doing programs right; they just need to regroup and re-gear their programming efforts.

Author Thom Rainer has studied program churches that have re-grouped and then relaunched in new and successful directions. He calls these churches "breakout churches." Many of these churches have been hindered and are in decline because of poor leadership, conflict, building space issues, or a moral failure. Rainer offers help to leaders of this kind of church in his book *Breakout Churches: Discover How to Make the Leap*. His book focuses on churches that have made the leap out of mediocrity to effectiveness.[8]

Highview Baptist Church in Louisville, Kentucky, and First Baptist Church in Geneva, Illinois, are good examples of what can happen when program churches are guided under the right kind of leadership. Pastor Kevin Ezell at Highview and Pastor Brian Coffey at First Baptist Geneva have brought new life to their already-mature ministries by incorporating dynamic, visionary leadership and a multicampus model.

Both Highview and First Baptist Church operate one church in multiple locations. Retaining and building on the strength of the more traditional main campus, these leaders have launched new locations using more contemporary ministry models. What makes this multicampus ministry approach viable is the strong base upon which these leaders have built their strategy. In a rather short time by church growth standards, both leaders were able to establish vibrant, growing ministries from churches that could instead have become relics.

The Power Church

Everyone has heard of the power church. It is contemporary, market savvy, and visionary. Like the pluralistic church we'll look at next, these churches seek to be culturally relevant as they desire to keep pace with the work of God's Spirit in the world. Led by baby boomer pastors, they believe anything is possible and plan to accomplish great things for God. As entrepreneurs, their leaders see the future and claim it for the gospel of Jesus Christ.

When you enter a power church you will notice some changes that have taken place from the church your mother attended. The facility looks more like an auditorium and less like a cathedral. Several massive screens allow for PowerPoint projection of the words of upbeat choruses (that sound an awful lot like the music I grew up on in the '60s, '70s and early '80s!). Nowhere in sight are hymnals or a pulpit, for that matter.

The stage is dominated by the equipment of the praise band. Sometime after they complete their set of songs, a Plexiglas podium is moved into position and the speaker, wired for sound with his nearly invisible microphone, takes center stage. The pastor looks more like Michael Eisner addressing an audience of Disney employees than a pastor or priest. Like Eisner, he is very polished, professional, and poised.

Relevant, needs-driven, and contemporary, this power church has taken that old gospel story and repackaged it for a new context. The church is massive and still growing. Using basic marketing strategies, it has become quite serious about taking the Great Commission for what it is—a charge to reach the world with the gospel message. By framing the message in a way that is attractive to the multitudes, this church is experiencing skyrocketing numerical growth. Following the principles of church growth experts, this church has found the right chemistry to attract many who would never set foot in a traditional church. This is no small accomplishment. At a time when the majority of Western churches are not seeing a single addition per year through conversion, this church is attracting an abundance of seekers. One thing is certain: Its purpose-driven strategy works.

Judging by the numbers, power churches are proven success stories. The most obvious examples are led by gifted individuals like Bill Hybels (pastor of Willow Creek Church in South Barrington, Illinois), Rick Warren (pastor of Saddleback Church in Lake Forest, California), Joel Osteen (pastor of Lakewood Church in Houston, Texas), and Bob Russell (pastor of Southeast Christian Church in Louisville, Kentucky). These are just four examples of leaders and their churches that fit this quadrant. They lead four of the megachurches that have sprung up across the country.

In 2003, Forbes Magazine identified 740 churches in the megachurch category with an average attendance of 3,646.[9] But not every church in this quadrant is a megachurch. Networked by a common desire to reach lost people, many leaders of moderate-sized churches have adopted the strategies of Willow Creek, Saddleback, and other megachurches through conferences, books, and Web site resources. By far, Warren's book *The Purpose-Driven Church* and Bill Hybels' *Becoming a Contagious Christian*[10] are among the most influential in this regard.

Seeker-sensitive, evangelistic, growth-oriented, contemporary, visionary, inspiring, motivating, dynamic, and pragmatic are words often associated with the power church. Power churches are works-oriented in that they value action, not just the theoretical or the theological. They are spirit-oriented in that they desire to experience the power of God as He works to do mighty things through His people. They are led by gifted people whose vision includes reaching the current generation for Christ as the church seeks to "become all things to all men so that by all possible means [it] might save some" (1 Corinthians 9:22).

The strengths of the power church are quite evident. First, it is committed to reaching lost people with the gospel in a relevant manner. We can debate the legitimacy of its methods, but none can challenge the genuineness of its goals. Second, it correctly understands the need to contextualize the message of Christ. Seeing their immediate communities as their mission field, the power church uses the methods of the missiologist to capture the interest of those who are seeking. Third, the power church must be commended for its cutting-edge spirit. It does not shy away from technology or methodology that is contemporary just to keep people who are already in the pews comfortable. Seizing the day is what the power church is about. And fourth, it is powerful in its actual impact. Its vision-driven leaders have affected people at all levels of our culture and have reached into settings that have otherwise been closed to evangelical influence.

When it comes to weaknesses, the power churches have received significant criticism. Many have challenged the marketing model as too business-driven, worldly, and compromising. They accuse the power church of dumbing down the message in order to reach unchurched Harry and Mary by focusing on felt needs rather than sin and righteousness. They have challenged the power church for perceived doctrinal weaknesses and exegetical error. Concerned that exposition of Scripture has been surrendered to entertainment, they often argue that the purpose-driven approach has subverted or at least trivialized the gospel.

Lastly, the power church has been criticized as being plastic, prepackaged, and nonauthentic. I can't tell you how many times I have heard Willow Creek described by critics as "a mile wide and one inch deep." In my own judgment, such criticism lacks a full awareness of what is actually happening at Willow Creek and other churches like it and of the many lives they have touched for Christ.

The Pluralistic Church

The houselights came down to the point of nearly complete darkness and then the music began. A discordant piece was played on the piano with great artistic flair. The music created a sense of turmoil and tension with its inharmonious and dark feel. Almost immediately the pastor, holding a single candle before her, began to walk slowly up the center aisle while singing the words, "He is the light of the world." Several times she repeated the phrase in a High Church style. The service continued with liturgy, the Apostles' Creed, a very contemporized Scripture recitation and a "reflection" from the pastor, rather than a sermon. That was last Christmas Eve and the place was a very postmodern church in Chicago's Gold Coast area. There were possibly seventy to one hundred people in attendance, maybe a few more. It was truly a diverse group, including young and old, wealthy and poor, black and white.

I was left with three impressions from this experience. First, I was struck by the minimal role of the Bible in the worship experience. The reflections of the pastor were only loosely linked to the Scriptures. The Scriptures were primarily presented in an artistic format with no direct reference to them or instruction in their meaning. Any use of the Bible was narrative in nature and nonpropositional in communication mode.

The second impression was that this was a highly existential experience. The goal was to create an experience for the congregation and teach through that experience. It felt like a curious blend of the first and twenty-first centuries. From my perspective, it would appeal to more artsy types and less so to those who tend toward an analytical understanding of their faith. Finally, it struck me as highly relevant to the postmodern person, many of whom populate downtown Chicago.

Though not all pluralistic churches are like the one I just described, most share some common characteristics. These are spirit-oriented and faith-oriented churches. As such they seek personal experiences in the spiritual realm and are highly reflective with regard to the matter of faith. These churches are often personal and relational in nature. They value a genuine experience of Christian community and their participants long for a deep encounter with God. These churches are places where all people are readily accepted, and where diversity of views and experiences are respected, valued, and encouraged. In many ways these churches offer personalized pastoral care, have a strong concern for matters of justice for the poor and downtrodden, and are places where each person's story or journey of faith matters.

Not all churches in the spirit- and faith-oriented, pluralistic quadrant are emergent churches, but emergent churches are rightly categorized in this quadrant. Authors like Richard Foster, Eddie Gibbs, Tony Jones, Dan Kimball, Brian McLaren, Erwin McManus, Leonard Sweet, Pete Ward, Dallas Willard, and Robert Webber are shaping this quadrant in this era. Theologians like Stanley Grenz, Karl Barth, and Reinhold Niebuhr define its beliefs. Pastors like Dan Kimball (Vintage Faith Church in Santa Cruz, California), Doug Pagitt (Solomon's Porch in Minneapolis), Mark Driscoll (Mars Hill Church in Seattle), and Rob Bell (Mars Hill Bible Church in Grand Rapids), are just a few of the leaders of this pluralistic arm of the church.

Other churches, not emergent in their associations, can also be classified here. These are typically smaller works, family-like in their environmental context, and many times parish-like in their ministry model. The distinguishing qualities of all churches in the pluralistic quadrant are highly relational ministry, nonjudgmental attitudes, a desire for a true sense of community, acceptance of fringe people, and authenticity in their quest for a personal encounter with Christ.

What are the strengths and weaknesses of this quadrant? The strengths certainly include a correct desire for community, authenticity, and an encounter with God.

The weaknesses are most often theological in nature due to their neo-orthodox and existential approach to the authority of Scripture. Most markedly, this pluralistic church is weak in its theological purity. It is a mixed bag to say the least—though most in this quadrant would consider that a compliment, not a criticism.

By far, the most significant criticism of churches in this quadrant has been the willingness to place spiritual experience before Scripture. This shows itself in a tolerance for concepts that are blatantly unbiblical and an unwillingness to take clear stands on biblically clear matters. Criticisms include a lack of commitment to the exclusivity of the gospel, full divinity and humanity of Christ, the authority of Scripture, and the clear teaching of Scripture concerning social issues such as homosexuality. Churches in this quadrant often will not take an unambiguous position. Because of the desire to be culturally relevant, this quadrant risks becoming culturally indistinct.

FROM THE MARGINS TO THE MIDDLE:
LEADING TOWARD BALANCED PRIORITIES

We have a trampoline in our backyard. Honestly, it is a bear to set up, so I have decided to leave it up all year long. I really don't care anymore if it rusts! Oh, right, back to my point—setting up that trampoline requires installing springs all the way around the frame to create an equal tension in all directions. You see, it is only when that tension is maintained that the trampoline works as designed. If I were to get lazy and only install springs on one-fourth, two-fourths, or even three-fourths of the circle, that trampoline will not perform properly.

I am convinced that the task of the leader-teacher is to create and maintain a similar kind of tension in church ministry. It is our job to maintain the spirit-truth and faith-works dynamic. Figure 8-4 depicts the concept graphically for us.

Table 8-4
THE PRIORITY-FOCUSED CHURCH

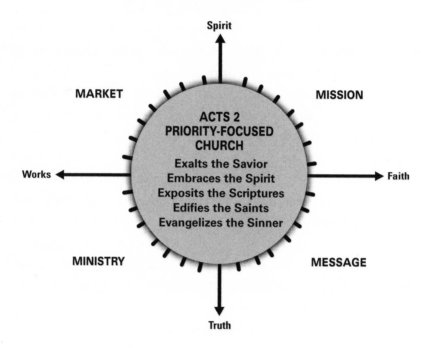

The Priority-Focused Church: Acts 2:1–47

Acts 2 is a remarkable account of the birth of the first-century church. In a post-resurrection appearance, Jesus had instructed his disciples to go to Jerusalem to await the empowerment of the Holy Spirit (Acts 1:8). Acts 2 records that event and its effects.

In the opening verses of chapter 2 we read of an amazing spiritual experience, a true encounter with the Spirit of God and His people.

> When the day of Pentecost came, they were all together in one place. Suddenly a sound like the blowing of a violent wind came from heaven and filled the whole house where they were sitting. They saw what seemed to be tongues of fire that separated and came to rest on each of them. All of them were filled with the Holy Spirit and began to speak in other tongues as the Spirit enabled them. (vv. 1–4)

Imagine seeing this. You hear the sound of a violent wind, see tongues of fire resting on the believers present, and then they begin to speak in foreign languages, unknown to the speaker but understood by those present. God-fearing Jews from all around the world were present, and they heard these men speak in their own languages. It must have been quite an experience. So bewildering was the experience, some began to wonder if the believers were merely drunk.

> Amazed and perplexed, they asked one another, "What does this mean?" Some, however, made fun of them and said, "They have had too much wine." (vv. 12–13)

This is when Peter addresses the crowd. He stands with the eleven disciples and explains the spiritual experience they just witnessed by teaching from the Word of God.

> Then Peter stood up with the Eleven, raised his voice and addressed the crowd: "Fellow Jews and all of you who live in Jerusalem, let me explain this to you; listen carefully to what I say. These men are not drunk, as you suppose. It's only nine in the morning! No, this is what was spoken by the prophet Joel." (Acts 2:14–16)

Here is an important observation. A spiritual encounter was not enough. That experience needed a logical explanation and interpretation based on God's Word. Experience alone is open to misinterpretation, which is exactly what happened here. Observers misunderstood the work of God as the work of wine. Peter had to "explain" or teach them the meaning of this experience from the propositional and reliable teachings of Scripture. Peter expounded on the Scriptures and showed how the prophets had predicted this day and how Jesus was, in fact, the fulfillment of the messianic promises of the Old Testament. Once they heard the Scriptures taught with clarity, it is interesting what occurs next. We are told that God moved in the lives of these listeners through the Word of God taught in power.

> When the people heard this, they were cut to the heart and said to Peter and the other apostles, "Brothers, what shall we do?" (v. 37)

Seeing that they had hearts that were open and a willingness to respond, Peter went on to present a very direct call to repentance and faith in Christ. We read:

> Peter replied, "Repent and be baptized, every one of you, in the name of Jesus Christ for the forgiveness of your sins. And you will receive the gift of the Holy Spirit. The promise is for you and your children and for all who are far off—for all whom the Lord our God will call." With many other words he warned them; and he pleaded with them, "Save yourselves from this corrupt generation." Those who accepted his message were baptized, and about three thousand were added to their number that day. (vv. 38–41)

Over three thousand people were added to the first band of believers. Clearly God was at work. His Spirit had come in power as Jesus had promised. What is more, the lives of these early believers were altered in very practical ways. We learn about this spiritual influence in verses 42–47.

> They devoted themselves to the apostles' teaching and to the fellowship, to the breaking of bread and to prayer. Everyone was filled with awe, and many wonders and miraculous signs were done by the apostles. All the believers were together and had everything in common. Selling their possessions and goods, they gave to anyone as he had need. Every day they continued to meet together in the temple courts. They broke bread in their homes and ate together with glad and sincere hearts, praising God and enjoying the favor of all the people. And the Lord added to their number daily those who were being saved. (vv. 42–47)

It is not uncommon to hear these final verses of Acts 2 presented as purpose statements for the church. We are told that the church should be determined to teach, pray, serve, fellowship, worship, and evangelize. But that is a misreading of the passage. These are not the *purpose* of the church; these are the *product* of the work of the Spirit of God and the Word of God in the church. The apostles did not decide to make these things happen; they faithfully cooperated with God's Spirit by doing that which they were called to do—teach.

What we do learn from this passage is something about the priorities of the first-century church. Dr. Danny Akin, president of Southeastern Baptist Theological Seminary in Wake Forest, North Carolina, identified these priorities. He describes the Acts 2 church as a church that: 1) exalted the Savior, 2) embraced the Spirit, 3) exposited the Scriptures, 4) edified the saints, and 5) evangelized the sinner.[11] Akin is on the money as he calls the twenty-first-century church back to the priorities of the first-century church of Acts 2.

The Leader-Teacher's Task

Your task as the leader-teacher is threefold. First, you must discover which quadrant most accurately describes the church you are called to lead. Second, you must exercise a style of ministry that is appropriate to that ministry context. And third, you must lead the people of God through a teaching ministry toward a more balanced emphasis on those priorities consistent with the Acts 2 church. Each of these types of churches we have studied in this chapter has characteristics that are positive, and each has potentially negative qualities. Leader-teachers must discern these and then find a healthy balance. Keep in mind that we are not to be either truth or Spirit, but both. Nor are we to be either faith or works, but again, we are to be both. Healthy churches actually maintain a tension between the ends of the continuums. That tension is found in a biblically balanced teaching ministry.

SPIRIT-TRUTH ASSESSMENT

Instructions: For each pair of descriptors, place a check mark by the one that best describes your church. Then count the check marks in each column.

Atmosphere	☐ casual, relaxed, informal	☐ structured, reserved, formal
Preaching	☐ devotional, inspirational	☐ doctrinal, interpretation-focused
Music	☐ contemporary	☐ traditional
Teaching	☐ application-oriented	☐ information-oriented
Emphasis	☐ feelings	☐ facts
Authority	☐ personal experiences	☐ scriptural teachings
Structure	☐ free-flowing	☐ orderly
Worship	☐ expressive, spontaneous	☐ controlled, preplanned
Decision making	☐ intuitive decisions	☐ logical decisions
Relationships	☐ easy to get to know others	☐ hard to get to know others
Change	☐ rapid	☐ slow
Strength	☐ worship experience	☐ commitment to Scripture

Other
Descriptors	☐ intuition	☐ information
	☐ encounter with God	☐ theology of God
Which	☐ paradigm shifts	☐ unchanging ideals
word best		
describes		
your church?	☐ relevance	☐ biblical
	☐ mystical	☐ empirical
	☐ spiritual formation	☐ Christian education
	☐ authentic experience	☐ authority over experience
	☐ subjective	☐ objective
	☐ cultural accommodation	☐ supracultural absolutes
	☐ immanence of God	☐ transcendence of God
	(God's presence)	(God's greatness)
	☐ expressive	☐ structured
	☐ community of believers	☐ commitment of the believer

Total Column 1 _____ **(Spirit-Orientation Score)**
Total Column 2 _____ **(Truth-Orientation Score)**
Based on observations, I would conclude that our church is _____ -oriented.

WORKS-FAITH ASSESSMENT

Instructions: For each pair of descriptors, place a check mark by the one that best describes your church. Then count the check marks in each column.

Our church is more............................	☐ active	☐ reflective
Our church is best described as more............................	☐ doing	☐ thinking
Our church's leadership could be described as.................................	☐ telling	☐ asking
Our church would be considered by visitors to be................................	☐ practical	☐ intellectual
Our church could be described as more................................	☐ practice oriented	☐ theory oriented
Our church is more............................	☐ evangelical	☐ instructive
Our church is marked by..................	☐ committees and boards	☐ small groups
Our church is more............................	☐ program-centered	☐ people-centered
Our church is more characterized by..............................	☐ involvement	☐ interaction
Our church would judge a person's commitment level by.........	☐ the extent of his/her involvement in church activities	☐ the depth of his/her personal relationships
Our church members are................	☐ pragmatic and practical	☐ scholarly and intellectual
Our church usually meets needs through...................................	☐ well-designed programs and ministries	☐ spontaneous ministry between people
Our church is more............................	☐ task oriented	☐ reflection oriented
Our church is more given to............	☐ doing	☐ contemplation
Our church places more value on..	☐ achievement	☐ relationships
Our church is....................................	☐ purpose-driven	☐ process-driven
Our church sees growth as.............	☐ size	☐ maturity
Our church is more like....................	☐ an organization	☐ a living organism
Our church is more like....................	☐ an enterprise	☐ a family

Total Column 1 _____ (Works-Orientation Score)
Total Column 2 _____ (Faith-Orientation Score)
Based on observations, I would conclude that our church is _____ -oriented.

Chapter Nine

FINISHING THE COURSE:
THE CHALLENGES OF THE LEADER-TEACHER

Guard what has been entrusted to your care. Turn away from godless chatter and the opposing ideas of what is falsely called knowledge, which some have professed and in so doing have wandered from the faith.

—1 Timothy 6:20–21

YOU have been entrusted with a great responsibility. The task of the leader-teacher is a high calling for which you are accountable. It is a noble task, but it is also a duty not to be taken lightly. Teachers must be cautious because they can easily become intoxicated with the power they have to influence the minds and hearts of others. Though we may not even realize it at the moment we teach, we do, in fact, shape others and through them, still others also.

As we began this book, we end it by proclaiming that some of the most powerful people in human history have been teachers. By facilitating change in people, teachers change not only the individual, but every person that that individual influences as well. Examples of such influence can be found in many stories about great teachers, but one in particular drives home that thought quite clearly.

You are probably familiar with Maria Montessori. She was, of course, the renowned educator who developed the method of instruction named for her and was the inspirational force behind the Montessori school movement. While her method is subject to evaluation and critique, few would deny the impact she has had on child-centered education.

It is likely you are less familiar with the person whose teaching influenced Maria. His name was Jean Marc Gaspard Itard. Itard was a great teacher whose influence cast a long shadow in the field of education. Though relatively unknown compared to Montessori, his impact was no less noteworthy. What made him so significant? He had credibility—credibility that caused Maria to take note of his teaching concepts as she read of his educational ideals. It was a credibility gained from being a man of character, compassion, and competency in his teaching efforts.

In 1799, Itard was a twenty-five-year-old physician living in Paris. Near the end of that year, Itard heard the remarkable story of a young "wild boy" who was sighted wandering in the woods near Saint Sernin sur Rance, in southern France. Itard read with interest of the boy's brief capture, his subsequent escape, and his eventual recapture. The boy, who had become known as "Victor," reemerged from the woods near the French town of Aveyron.

On the cold morning of January 9, 1800, the residents of the village were confronted with a strange creature who walked erect but in all other ways appeared as an animal. Hair matted and long, covered with dirt and unclothed, the very short boy appeared as if he had just stepped out of ancient history. Unable to speak, he was limited to wild animal-like sounds, emitting a few weird cries of apparent fear. During the night the boy had approached the garden of a tanner where he began to dig up vegetables. In his quest for enough food to survive, he was recaptured. Soon the entire village heard of the boy and turned out in great numbers to see the child. Because the people were bewildered by his appearance and tendencies, this young boy was the focus of immediate debate. Was he human? Was he an animal? Was he some kind of wild savage?

Taken by the gendarmes, the "savage boy" was first brought to a hospice for orphans where he remained for a month. Then he was taken to a laboratory for scientific study, as Victor became the focus of scholarly and scientific debate. Victor's discovery occurred during the historical period of the Enlightenment. It was a time when human reason reigned supreme and when science replaced religion and the church as the primary authority with regard to defining the nature of truth.

During this period, controversy raged about what exactly separates humans from animals. Victor was an ideal experimental subject for scientists eager to test their theories of human nature. The boy became the focal point of an immense debate in France between the "nativists," who believed that a person's potential was determined by genetic heritage and was therefore unalterable; and the "sensationists," who believed that environmental input in the form of sensory experience could change a person's intellectual development. Who would venture to teach this "wild boy"? Who would dare to "civilize" him?

Moved with a deep sense of compassion and even more deeply held values regarding the worth and dignity of people, Itard stepped forward and volunteered to raise the boy. Itard wanted to teach him to speak and aid him in learning some basic human relationship skills. For five years, he and the boy lived together at the school for deaf children in Paris while Itard attempted to teach him. His ultimate hope was that the child would learn verbal communication skills, which Itard considered the principal trait of civilized persons. Through daily lessons, Itard worked with Victor to teach him foundational life skills. Despite Itard's dedication, it took nine months before Victor had accomplished even the most basic goals of Itard's instruction: normal eating, sleeping, and personal hygiene routines.

After five years, Itard became discouraged. He had made little progress. He was distressed for the boy and felt his work on the boy's behalf was a failure. Victor could recognize some words in print and had acquired some basic skills, but his only words were *lait* and *oh Dieu* (French for "milk" and "oh God"). With great disappointment, Itard surrendered the care of Victor to the wife of a groundskeeper at the school.

He felt she was better able to meet the boy's need for love and affection. Victor lived with this family until his death at around the age of forty.

Although Itard considered himself a failure, others found his teaching techniques to be innovative. In all likelihood, Victor was autistic. What Itard had demonstrated was that progress could be made with individuals who have severe learning disabilities. Driven by a virtuous character and compassion, his efforts with Victor gave many people encouragement that even those with severe disabilities and who have been forgotten by society could be helped to learn.

Edward Seguin was one of those who saw potential in Itard's teaching theory. Seguin was a student of Itard. Building on Itard's methods, Seguin formed his own ideas about teaching children with profound learning disabilities. Seguin wrote of Itard's novel methods in a book later translated by Maria Montessori. As she translated, she came to believe that Itard's work had credibility even though his results were not as he had hoped. Thus, through the teaching of Itard and through the writing of Seguin came the Montessori method, a teaching method that values the student's natural curiosity.[1]

Stories like this remind us of the power of teachers. It is the power to shape future generations. Christa McAuliffe, the famed teacher in space, died in 1986 when the space shuttle *Challenger* exploded just 73 seconds after liftoff, killing all seven astronauts aboard. Before the launch, Christa was asked about her life passion. Her response was framed in her now-famous words: "I touch the future—I teach." In a real sense, while her travels to space as the first civilian on the shuttle may have ended tragically, her life's work as a teacher continues. Christa was an example to young people of dedication and personal sacrifice. After her death, following her example and motivated by her words, many young people entered the teaching profession.

Teachers do have power—power to influence the future by influencing their students and even those who come after them. As James Means put it, "An excellent teacher fashions better people and, ultimately, a different society."[2] This is, in fact, why Paul called Timothy to entrust the teaching he had received from Paul "to reliable men who will also be qualified to teach others" (2 Timothy 2:2). Those who plan to touch the future through teaching God's Word must consider four challenges that face every biblical leader-teacher. How we handle these challenges determines whether we succeed or fail at this calling.

THE CHALLENGE OF ORTHODOXY

Leader-teachers need to be aware just how easy it is to drift off course theologically. In fact, it is far easier to drift off course than it is to remain on course. When one is sailing or flying to a destination, there is just one vector that will take you to your objective. Many routes may seem appealing for a time, but continuing on them will bring disappointment and could even bring ruin. Using the image of narrow and broad roads, Jesus taught this principle to His followers. In Matthew's gospel we read the words of Jesus.

> Enter through the narrow gate. For wide is the gate and broad is the road that leads to destruction, and many enter through it. But small is the gate and narrow the road that leads to life, and only a few find it. (Matthew 7:13–14)

His words carry a somber warning to His listeners. But He does not end His call to orthodox belief with this image. He continued to warn of "false prophets" who stealthily move in amid God's people for the purpose of ravaging them like wolves among sheep.

> Watch out for false prophets. They come to you in sheep's clothing, but inwardly they are ferocious wolves. By their fruit you will recognize them. (Matthew 7:15–16)

As his mentor and instructor in the ministry, Paul warned Timothy of the risks of drifting from orthodox belief.

> Timothy, my son, I give you this instruction in keeping with the prophecies once made about you, so that by following them you may fight the good fight, holding on to faith and a good conscience. Some have rejected these and so have shipwrecked their faith. (1 Timothy 1:18–20)

If we don't stay on course, we run a real risk of shipwrecking our faith.

One of the challenges that teachers face is remaining orthodox in their theology and committed to the authority of Scripture. Let's face it—false teachers are generally highly capable and knowledgeable teachers who, for some reason, have gone astray in their thinking but are still appealing. That is why, despite their errors in theology, they are attractive to their learners. They are convincing to weaker, younger believers. Peter warns of them in no uncertain terms and is clear about the disrepute they bring to the message of the truth and about their eventual ends.

> But there were also false prophets among the people, just as there will be false teachers among you. They will secretly introduce destructive heresies, even denying the sovereign Lord who bought them— bringing swift destruction on themselves. Many will follow their shameful ways and will bring the way of truth into disrepute. In their greed these teachers will exploit you with stories they have made up. Their condemnation has long been hanging over them, and their destruction has not been sleeping. (2 Peter 2:1–3)

Peter is not alone in his warnings about false teachers. We hear of false teachers in several places in Scripture. Paul warned of their activity in Acts 20 when he met with the elders of the church at Ephesus. He instructed them,

> Keep watch over yourselves and all the flock of which the Holy Spirit has made you overseers. Be shepherds of the church of God,

which he bought with his own blood. I know that after I leave, savage wolves will come in among you and will not spare the flock. Even from your own number men will arise and distort the truth in order to draw away disciples after them. So be on your guard! (Acts 20:28–31)

As leader-teachers it is imperative that we remain faithful to an orthodox faith and teaching—faith that was "once for all delivered to the saints" (Jude 1:3 NKJV). James could not be clearer on this point. "Not many of you should presume to be teachers, my brothers, because you know that we who teach will be judged more strictly" (James 3:1). In the verses that follow, James goes on to explain the power of the tongue, the teacher's primary means of communication. But he could have just as easily spoken of the written word as well. Words are powerful and teachers are wordsmiths. As such, they must be cautious that they teach only and always the truth of Scripture, regardless of the medium they select. It is God's Word, faithfully taught, that holds authority and with it the power to change lives.

In this book I have raised a number of concerns with regard to the emergent church movement. Here is a good place to be abundantly clear. It is not the methodology of these postmodern Christians that troubles me, but the clear drift from orthodoxy, especially with regard to the authority of Scripture. We cannot afford "a generous orthodoxy" that is, as Albert Mohler puts it, "so generous that it ceases to be orthodox.³" Mohler continues,

> The Emergent movement represents a significant challenge to biblical Christianity. Unwilling to affirm that the Bible contains propositional truths that form the framework for Christian belief, this movement argues that we can have Christian symbolism and substance without those thorny questions of truthfulness that have so vexed the modern mind. The worldview of postmodernism—complete with an epistemology that denies the possibility of or need for propositional truth—affords the movement an opportunity to hop, skip and jump

throughout the Bible and the history of Christian thought in order to take whatever pieces they want from one theology and attach them, like doctrinal post-it notes, to whatever picture they would want to draw.[4]

Mohler's evaluation is correct and his concern is rightly placed. As leader-teachers we must tenaciously avoid this drift from orthodoxy. Some emergent leaders today have drifted from historical orthodoxy toward a neo-orthodoxy and further to philosophical existentialism. Others have more subtly drifted toward pragmatism. Still others have drifted so far off course that they have run aground on the rocks of agnosticism, abandoning their commitment to the authority of the Scriptures altogether.

WHAT HAPPENED TO ART? That was my question when I heard a former classmate of mine interviewed by NPR (National Public Radio). Art appeared as a guest to discuss his most recent book. It is a book designed to undermine confidence in the Bible as the Word of God. Art is now a self-described agnostic. But he wasn't always as uncertain of the truthfulness of Scripture and its authority as God's Word. There was a time in his life that he embraced orthodox theology. When I had heard that he had renounced his evangelical roots in favor of agnosticism, I became curious to hear Art's own account of what happened to him to cause the change. The host asked him, "In a recent article you wrote, you said that you consider yourself an agnostic now. What was the turning point for you to actually deciding that that's what you were—an agnostic?" Here is his response.

> It was a long process for me because I had gone from being a social oriented Episcopalian to being an ultraconservative evangelical. I guess basically I was a fundamentalist for several years. But then my views started changing. I moved into liberal Christianity and then I started doubting just about everything, even the things the Bible talks about. . . .
>
> And, eventually after thinking about issues for years and years, and

knowing the problems in the Bible, and knowing that my faith had been rooted in the words of the Bible, which I couldn't trust any longer because I wasn't sure we even had the words. All of these things combined to eventually make me think that maybe I didn't believe anymore. And so, it was only seven or eight years ago that I began calling myself an agnostic. . . .

It is better now because I no longer believe something that I know to be false. The words of the Bible are not the inerrant words from God. There are discrepancies in the Bible that cannot be reconciled and we don't even have the original words themselves. And so basing one's life on words that we don't even have doesn't seem like the best way to go.[5]

It is important for the leader-teacher to remain orthodox in theological commitment since the goal of leading through teaching is having an influence on others. Leader-teachers carry an enormous responsibility in this role. Drifting from orthodoxy is easy. The challenge for the leader-teacher is to remain on course.

THE CHALLENGE OF AUTHENTICITY

Meeting the challenge of authenticity sounds simple, but is actually quite involved.

The word *authentic* means "conforming to fact and therefore worthy of trust, reliance, or belief."[6] Synonyms for the word *authentic* include genuine, real, vulnerable, honest, trustworthy, and bona fide. Biblical leader-teachers must seek to retain an authentic relationship with followers. Authenticity flows out of a genuine and deepening relationship with Christ, an honest awareness of oneself (strengths and weaknesses alike), a vulnerability in living one's faith with fellow believers (warts and all), trust expressed in listening to and empowering others, and a bona fide love for people as they are at the moment. Sounds pretty simple, but it really is not in our nature to be authentic.

We often put forward the face we want others to see or the one we think they want to see. The truth is, the best of leaders among us are not perfect, but they are vulnerable and appropriately transparent about their own limitations and growth process. What makes authentic leaders most effective is that they have already been where their followers are going and they remember the challenges that followers will face.

Authenticity is not perfection, but it does come from testing. Life challenges and difficulties form character, and authentic leaders are those who have come through those experiences with their faith intact. Authentic leaders do not have an attitude of moral superiority and are not hypocritical. They are a living demonstration that, despite the struggles of life in this world, it is possible to live faithfully for Christ. In the 1820s and 1830s a breed of men arose in the West known as the mountain men. Mountain men were rugged people who set out into the Rockies to trap fur, explore, and seek adventure. By the time settlers moved West in the 1850s and '60s, these people knew the mountains so well they served as guides to help "flatlanders" traverse the canyons and heights of Colorado and Wyoming. They were trusted for their knowledge, for they possessed the secrets of experiences. They were given enormous credibility with followers because they had an authentic knowledge of the terrain, perils, and safe passages.

Authentic leadership is something like that. It is gained from having traversed the path. Serving as a guide and pilgrim, the authentic leader-teacher goes ahead and then, when the way is certain, calls others to follow.

Authentic leadership involves serving as a humble example. It means being the genuine article, the real thing. Such authenticity stands in opposition to that which is false, fabricated, or counterfeit. Authentic leader-teachers are what they purport to be. They are credible because they are reliable and trustworthy.

THE CHALLENGE OF HUMILITY

What is the opposite of humility? Words like superiority, vanity, narcissistic, arrogant, prideful, boastful come to mind. Arrogance seems to announce itself. The evidence of arrogant leadership includes leaders who step into a new setting and fail to acknowledge what had been accomplished in the past, who fail to match their leadership style to the context, or who speak and act with an attitude of condescension.

People are instinctively repulsed by these qualities. Leader-teachers must wrestle the demon of pride and vanity to the ground if they are to succeed in their role as a biblical leader using the vehicle of teaching to shape lives.

The greatest threat to humility is—success. When leader-teachers gain a following because of their effectiveness as a communicator or because of the growth of the ministry they lead, they must take caution. The great risk of success is a growing narcissism. Narcissism is an excessive love or admiration of oneself. Conceit, arrogance, and egocentrism are all synonyms for this tendency.

Notice that we are talking about an "excessive" love or admiration. A well-reasoned self-concept is appropriate and empowering, but an excessive admiration of self brings a lack of humility and the loss of teaching effectiveness, at least for those who seek to teach like Jesus. Paul called believers to "Do nothing out of selfish ambition or vain conceit, but in humility consider others better than yourselves. Each of you should look not only to your own interests, but also to the interests of others" (Philippians 2:3–4).

Paul then illustrates his point by the ultimate example of humility and selflessness, Jesus Christ (Philippians 2:5–11). Step by step, Paul describes Jesus' surrender of His personal rights leading Him from the throne room of heaven, to a stable, and on to the cross. How are followers of Jesus to respond to others in light of Christ's example? He says, "Your attitude should be the same as that of Christ Jesus" (2:5). Such humility is a challenge to attain and to maintain, especially in a leadership and teaching role. For some leader-teachers, their self-confidence, self-assuredness, and charisma can, in fact, be their Achilles' heel.

Many years ago, a researcher into human personality theorized that four differing personality types exist in each person, with one quality dominating the others. Based on his research, he identified four distinct personality types. These four characteristics help further our understanding of the challenge of humility.

This researcher identified the first characteristic of human personality as the need to give and receive love. The researcher concluded that all of us desire to extend loving care to others and that when we do, we find a measure of personal pleasure in the response we receive in return. Although this trait is found in virtually every person, the researcher discovered that people who were dominated by this quality tend to be outwardly focused and often become teachers, nurses, social workers, counselors, and many other service-related, people-centered professionals.

The second characteristic he observed is a tendency in all of us to be obsessive about some matters. This obsessive quality actually is a positive thing, for it is the quality that makes us self-disciplined, self-reliant, and conscientious. Used in a positive way, this characteristic to be obsessive can propel the individual to excellence in an area. For example, to be a professional athlete or compete at the level of an Olympian, a person must become obsessive about the athletic pursuit. Most of us lack that level of obsessive dedication, but we do have enough of the quality to be excellent at something.

But on the flip side, for those dominated by this obsessive quality, life can become inwardly directed. Misdirected obsessions can be dangerous. Obsessive types can become perfectionists or they can become so disconnected from others by their obsessions that they end up living isolated lives. Taken to the extreme, highly obsessive people will often trade relationships for the sake of their obsessions.

The third characteristic observed by the researcher was the tendency to become similar to those we are around. Most of us want to fit in, so we tend to change to some degree with the group we are a part of at any given moment. The researcher observed this trait in all people, but especially in persons he called "marketing types." When found with this characteristic in the extreme, marketing types seem to change with the direction of the wind. They lack their own opinions, values, and purpose. These unproductive marketing types lack direction and the ability to commit themselves to people or to projects. But when this trait is controlled and turned to productive purposes, marketing types can be effective at facilitating teams and providing wonderful customer service.

The fourth personality characteristic that the researcher identified was a tendency in all persons toward individuality and independence. This tendency involves independent thinking, necessary and moderate aggressiveness, self-confidence, and power. In some people this characteristic only shows up in their need to control the family dog, while others need to lead corporate empires or entire nations. When positively directed, this is the quality that makes one an entrepreneur, a risk-taker, a self-starter, innovator, goal-directed—a leader. But taken the wrong direction, this quality can be entirely self-serving and egocentric. The researcher called this quality *narcissism.*[7]

Narcissism is one of the challenges faced by the leader-teacher. On one hand, self-confidence can bring success to a leader, but over time it can evolve toward arrogance and self-promotion. While everyone is capable of narcissistic behaviors, some have this tendency to an extreme measure, which proves to be both a blessing and a curse.

In his award-winning article "Narcissistic Leaders: The Incredible Pros, the Inevitable Cons,"[8] author Michael Maccoby called these persons the "makers and shapers of our public and personal agendas" and the "visionary and charismatic" persons we tend to look to to lead us. Maccoby observed that,

> Throughout history, narcissists have always emerged to inspire people and to shape the future. When military, religious, and political

arenas dominated society, it was figures such as Napoléon Bonaparte, Mahatma Ghandi, or Franklin Delano Roosevelt who determined the social agenda. But from time to time, when business became the engine of social change, it, too, generated its share of narcissistic leaders. That was true at the beginning of this century, when men like Andrew Carnegie, John D. Rockefeller, Thomas Edison, and Henry Ford exploited new technologies and restructured American industry. And I think it is true again today.

He goes on to cite persons like Jack Welch, Bill Gates, Steve Jobs, and Larry Ellison. Maccoby observed that such leaders are respected as "personalities" and are celebrity types, writing best-selling books on how they led such-and-such company to success. But with these accolades come a downside. Maccoby observed that these narcissistic people many times are "emotionally isolated and highly distrustful. Perceived threats can trigger rage. Achievements can feed feelings of grandiosity."

Business is not alone in producing its powerhouse leaders. In the last few decades, evangelical Christianity has created a few of its own. Think a bit and you can probably name several. Many of these Christian leaders bring the self-confidence needed for success. Unfortunately, however, there are some who have been brought down by the negative aspects of narcissism. Narcissistic leaders bring the positive quality of self-confidence. But without the balance of those who are willing to challenge the visionary dreams of the narcissist with reality, narcissistic leaders run the risk of damaging their organizations. Maccoby writes,

> The challenge facing organizations is to ensure that such leaders do not self-destruct or lead the company to disaster. That can take some doing because it is very hard for narcissists to work through their issues—and virtually impossible for them to do it alone.

While narcissism in a leader can actually be a strength, as leaders they have some major weaknesses as well. These include sensitivity to criticism, poor listening skills, a lack of empathy, a distaste for mentoring, an intense need to compete, and in their later years, an excessive focus on personal legacy over and above organizational advancement.

To their credit, narcissistic leaders thrive on risk, have immense vision, and have scores of followers. If their weaknesses are controlled, these leaders can be enormously effective. But the solution to their weaknesses is accountability and the encouragement of a humble spirit. Until they accept such correction, these leaders will not maintain their teaching impact for a lifetime. Worse yet, narcissistic leaders can risk all of their achievements in a moment of personal gratification or, more subtly, in a less-than-stellar finish.

The monumental challenge then is one of humility. Great leader-teachers recognize the risks of pride and narcissism and take needed steps to avoid this leadership trap. They also know that it is only by the power of the Spirit of God that such humility is possible in times of great success.

THE CHALLENGE OF INTEGRITY

Integrity is about character and virtue. You will recall we examined those concepts in detail earlier in the book. But integrity is also about two other critically important matters—power and principles. Persons with integrity use, rather than abuse, power. Likewise, persons with integrity are principled individuals.

James Means makes a cogent observation with regard to the use of power in ministry. After recognizing that leadership entails influence and the use of power, he raises the question, "What is or is not appropriate use of that power? How much authority and power is appropriate for church leaders and to what extent are church leaders to be held accountable to their constituencies or to external authorities?"[9] He then writes,

Leaders have differed widely in their answer to these questions, depending upon their personal convictions, biblical interpretations, ecclesiastical traditions, and the sensitivity of their consciences. Many have a pragmatic approach that rather crassly suggests that a good end justifies virtually any means of achieving it. Some also have assumed that power should be gained to the extent allowed by followers. At the other extreme, there are those who have been so ethically tender that they have been reluctant to use any persuasive efforts; they have eschewed authority and, as a result, their effectiveness is minimal. Effectiveness requires influence, but spiritual leadership is limited by severe biblical constraints.[10]

According to authors French and Raven, power can be sorted into five distinct categories. How a leader uses these forms of power says a lot about their integrity. Research by Gary A. Yukl, State University of New York at Albany, studied each of these five types of power in detail (table 9-1). He concluded that effective leaders rely on personal power more than they do position power, though position power is still important. But knowledge alone about the use of power is not enough to define how leader-teachers should incorporate power in their ministries.

Integrity demands that we use power only in ways consistent with the limitations of Scripture and those options Scripture leaves open to us. For example, Scripture forbids us from "lording it over others." Jesus made that point abundantly clear when He said,

> Jesus called them together and said, "You know that the rulers of the Gentiles lord it over them, and their high officials exercise authority over them. Not so with you. Instead, whoever wants to become great among you must be your servant, and whoever wants to be first must be your slave— just as the Son of Man did not come to be served, but to serve, and to give his life as a ransom for many. (Matthew 20:25–28)

Likewise, Peter instructs elders to shepherd the flock, "not lording it over those entrusted to you, but being examples to the flock" (1 Peter 5:3). Lording it over another is position power that incorporates

Table 9-1
POWER TAXONOMY

Type of Power[11]	Description[12]
Reward power	The target person complies in order to obtain rewards he or she believes are controlled by the agent.
Coercive power	The target person complies in order to avoid punishments he or she believes are controlled by the agent.
Legitimate power	The target person complies because he or she believes the agent has the right to make the request and the target person has the obligation to comply.
Expert power	The target person complies because he or she believes that the agent has special knowledge about the best way to do something.
Referent power	The target person complies because he or she admires or identifies with the agent and wants to gain the agent's approval.

fear and threat. Such use of power demonstrates a lack of integrity in the leader.

Coercive power can also be problematic. If leaders use manipulation, politics, and bribery, they are clearly out of bounds. But coercive power can be far more subtle. For example, a leader I once worked with sought support for a beloved program by proclaiming to a committee, "If any of you vote against this, you will certainly be out of fellowship with God. I know this is God's will for He gave me the vision for this ministry." That kind of spiritual power play forces the follower into a no-win situation. Fortunately, the members of that committee saw through the effort to sway them with spiritual blackmail and voted to no longer fund the ministry, which had run its course years before.

Integrity is evidenced in how one seeks to live out the principles he or she verbally embraces. The word "integrity" is the "quality or state of being whole and undivided."[13] The term is Latin in its origin and comes from the word *integratis*, which is where we get the math term *integer*. An integer is a whole number and thus, is not divided. A life of integrity is a life that matches one's principles. It is undivided. It is not compartmentalized. People who have integrity are the same person in any situation because they are driven by a set of core values or principles. Integrity in its finest example is found in the life of the Christian leader grounded on the truth of God's Word and not divided or compartmentalized. It is no compliment for someone to say that you are good at compartmentalizing your life. That could well be a statement that points to a lack of integrity.

"Integrity" was the most looked-up word of 2005, according to Merriam-Webster's online dictionary. It is little wonder, given the issues of political corruption that lead the news, including stories of bribes to congressmen from lobbyists. People long for leaders with integrity.

John Baptist de LaSalle was a remarkable man, a leader of unusual virtue and principle. Born into great rank and family fortune, John's life was marked from the beginning for aristocratic prominence. John, the eldest son of a French nobleman who lived in enormous wealth just outside of Paris, was born April 30, 1651. The great wealth of his family set a chasm between him and the impoverished masses of the poor living in Paris and the surrounding towns at the time. John was educated in the finest institutions from his youth and attended a prestigious college in his young adult years. Noticed by church leaders as a man of strong character, he was encouraged to enter the priesthood. He attended seminary and was considered a leading candidate for the highest of posts in his church's hierarchical system.

On one occasion during his seminary training, John was asked to help teach at a small school in his hometown. The school sought to teach children who lived in wretched poverty. The hope was that education might enable some to find work outside of the ghetto. John was intensely moved by the needs of the children he met and, at that moment, sensed

God's call upon his life. He knew that he was to give his life to teaching, whatever the cost.

But John not only recognized the poor conditions that plagued the lives of these children; he also observed the meager circumstances of the school itself and the great sacrifice its teachers were making to be there. These teachers had little training but had hearts devoted to their students. They lacked the means for a teacher's education, but made up for that deficiency by being utterly dedicated to their students' learning. In response to the needs he experienced at that school, John opened his own home to the school's teachers, inviting them to come and live with him. There he began to train them in teaching, starting a kind of teacher's college.

Against his family's wishes, John dedicated his life, not to a great position of leadership in the church, but to a lowly role as a teacher, principal, and teacher of teachers in a destitute urban school. At great personal sacrifice and with the extraordinary power of virtue-driven leadership, John de LaSalle vowed to invest all he had in money, time, health, and talent to build free schools for impoverished children.

In time, the teachers he trained went out to start other schools all around France and on into Switzerland and Italy. John was so successful in his free-school model of education that schoolmasters in the paid schools became infuriated. The best and the brightest of their schools, though not in poverty, were seeking entrance to John's schools. The result was that the paid schools were feeling the pinch in both dollars and scholars. In an effort to stop John's free-school movement, they sued John in the French courts and, for a time, were able to hinder the continuance of his work. But with the support of religious and political leaders, his schools were soon back in business under the auspices of his church.

John eventually established three colleges, which, in many ways, were the forerunners of modern institutions of a similar nature. With the help of the teachers he trained, as well as their students, John's educational efforts have endured to this day. Today there are over fifteen thousand members of the Brothers of the Christian Schools, established by John, leading schools of all kinds all around the world. John himself wrote three books on education, one of which became an educational classic, appearing in over a hundred editions.[14]

John was a man of principle who was willing to sacrifice everything so that he could teach. His principled life gave him credibility and influence that multiplied his impact and continues into the present. Such principled integrity teaches powerfully. Such principled integrity gives strength to the words of a leader-teacher.

A Concluding Thought

There have been many great leaders throughout history. They have inspired, guided, challenged, protected, and provoked us to achievements and victories we would not have accomplished without their vision and drive. But the greatest of these leaders have been the ones who have led by teaching. They were not the greatest because they were the most prominent or the most powerful. They were the greatest of leaders because their efforts produced changed lives and served to shape the future.

As one who now teaches each day, I am grateful to those who have faithfully taught me over the years. Sunday school teachers, elementary teachers, junior high school teachers, high school teachers, professors, pastors, and parents all have fashioned my life by their efforts. Precept upon precept, each one has built truth into my life in ways that have freed me and empowered me. For their efforts I am most thankful.

Today was a wonderful day in the classroom. I sensed again the privilege it is to stand before a room full of capable and energetic students and to serve them by guiding their discovery process. Today they interacted, they raised questions, and they participated. It is not always this good. Many times I wonder if I communicated anything or if they truly wrestled with anything we discussed. But today I will take joy in the moment while it is mine. You see, today I believe they encountered the truth in a fresh way and have discovered something they probably have not considered before.

This year marks my twentieth year at this teaching task, and I am more energized today by the prospect of teaching than ever before. And why not? What else can one do that has a more direct impact on people than to teach someone something that they will take with them forever? What's more, to see lives changed and then, through those students, to see others influenced—there is little that can bring more joy.

Today a student came up after class and said, "Dr. Bredfeldt, thanks, that was a fun class. It has been a long time since I have had so much fun learning." Another wrote me an e-mail recently saying, "Dr. Bredfeldt, your course has made me rethink how I communicate God's Word to others. I realize that I can't just deliver content; I must get people to internalize that content by engaging them in learning."

And finally, a third student said, "I now see my teaching ministry as my most important task in ministry leadership." Comments like those stoke the furnace of my teacher's heart.

This book has been a call to the ministry of teaching. It has been my desire to inform, inspire, challenge, and transform. It is my prayer that you will be encouraged to join me in this wonderful leadership venture called *teaching*. Yes, it is demanding. Without a doubt, it is challenging. In this chapter we considered just four of those challenges—the challenge of orthodoxy, the challenge of authenticity, the challenge of humility, and the challenge of integrity. These are no small obstacles, but it is the challenges of teaching that makes leading by teaching so exciting. You may not end up teaching thousands, hundreds, or even more than a handful of people, but the challenge remains just the same. Here is the encouraging news: If you choose to be a leader-teacher, regardless of the context or size of the audience, you will enter a divine partnership to accomplish God's purposes in this world.

And most rewarding of all, you will sense God's pleasure.

NOTES

Introduction

1. Timothy George, *Amazing Grace: God's Initiative—Our Response* (Nashville: LifeWay, 2000), 99.

2. This account of Mrs. Bartlett's ministry is summarized from a dissertation by Thomas Michael O'Neal Jr, "An Analysis of the Ministry of Charles H. Spurgeon with Implications for the Modern Church Growth Movement." (PhD diss., Southern Baptist Theological Seminary, 2006), 86–87.

Chapter 1

1. James P. Eicher, "Post-Heroic Leadership: Managing the Virtual Organization," http://www.pignc-ispi.com/articles/management/post-heroic.htm.

2. Eddie Gibbs, *LeadershipNext: Changing Leaders in a Changing Culture* (Downers Grove: InterVarsity) 2005, 39–43.

3. Peter M. Senge, *The Fifth Discipline* (New York: Currency Doubleday, 1994), 339–360.

4. Irving Janis, *Groupthink* (CRM Learning, 1996). In this training video, actors reconstruct the events that lead up to the *Challenger* disaster. Account is based on that video and Noel Tichy's reference to it in *The Cycle of Leadership*, 56.

5. John Maxwell, *Developing the Leader Within You* (Nashville: Thomas Nelson, 1993), 1.

6. http://homepage.mac.com/crabtree/msriley.htm.

7. Homer Hickam, *Rocket Boys* (New York: Delacorte Press, 1998). Produced by Larry Franco and Charles Gordon as *October Sky* in 1999 by Universal Pictures, directed by Joe Johnston.

8. Delivered on the steps at the Lincoln Memorial in Washington DC on August 28, 1963. Source: http://www.usconstitution.net/dream.html.

9. Noel M. Tichy, *The Cycle of Leadership: How Great Leaders Teach Their Companies to Win* (New York: Harper Business, 2004), 57.

10. Terry Pearce, *Leading Out Loud: Inspiring Change Through Authentic Communication* (San Francisco: Jossey-Bass, 2003), 45.

Chapter 3

1. Parker Palmer, *The Courage to Teach: Exploring the Inner Landscape of a Teacher's Life* (San Francisco: Jossey-Bass, 1997), 17.

2. The Emergent Church Movement (ECM) is a movement that embraces a neo-orthodox understanding of Scripture. Its leaders emphasize reading the Bible existentially and

experientially rather than expositorially and exegetically. It focuses on a narrative approach to the Bible and rejects the idea that the Bible is to be taught as absolute propositional truth. The ECM approaches Scripture in a postmodern way, similar to the way the U.S. constitution is approached by "interpretivists." Rather than seeking the natural, normal, original meaning of the text, ECM leaders encourage an encounter or experience with God in the text. While many aspects of the emergent church movement are positive, including a desire to be relevant in communicating the Bible, many evangelical scholars have concluded that the movement is rapidly moving away from the post-Reformational commitment of Protestants to the principle of *Sola Scriptura* or the Bible alone. For more information on emergent churches and the ECM, read D.A. Carson's book, *Becoming Conversant with the Emerging Church* (Zondervan).

3. http://leadlikejesus.com.

4. Laurie Beth Jones, *Jesus, CEO: Using Ancient Wisdom for Visionary Leadership* (New York: Hyperion, 1995).

5. John A. Byrne, "How Jack Runs GE," *Business Week*, June 8, 1998.

6. Ibid.

7. Ilion Jones, *The Pastor: The Man and His Ministry* (Philadelphia: Westminister, 1961), 63.

8. James E. Means, *Leadership in Christian Ministry* (Grand Rapids: Baker, 1989), 53–54.

9. J. Robert Clinton, *The Making of a Leader* (Colorado Springs: CO: NavPress, 1998), 17.

10. Donald L. Hughes, "The Leadership Model of Jesus." Accessed at http://www.Jesus Journal.com/content/view/90/85. Undated article.

11. Robert T. Kiyosaki and Sharon L. Lechter, *The Rich Dad's Guide to Investing* (New York: Warner Books, 2000), 393.

CHAPTER 4

1. Researcher George Barna has concluded that 86 percent of born-again Christians believe "the Bible is totally accurate in all of its teachings." He also found that just 32 percent of born-again Christians said they believe in moral absolutes. Source: The Barna Group website http://www.barna.org/FlexPage.aspx?Page=Topic&TopicID=8.

2. Richard R. Osmer, *A Teachable Spirit: Recovering the Teaching Office in the Church* (Philadelphia: Westminster/John Knox Press), 1990, 43.

3. Ibid., p. 44.

4. Ibid., p. 45.

5. Brian McLaren, author of *A Generous Orthodox* (Zondervan, 2004), *The Story We Find Ourselves In* (Jossey-Bass, 2003), *More Ready Than You Realize* (Zondervan, 2002), and *A New Kind of Christian* (Jossey-Bass, 2001), and a key leader in the emergent church movement, is case in point. Many other Christian postmodern authors could be cited as well, but McLaren's work is probably most widely read, quoted, and embraced by the emerging church movement.

6. Brian McLaren, *More Ready Than You Realize* (Grand Rapids: Zondervan, 2002), 94.

7. Brian McLaren, *A New Kind of Christian* (San Francisco: Jossey-Bass, 2001), 106.

8. Ibid., 70.

9. Available online at http://www.pbs.org/wgbh/pages/frontline/shows/jesus/evangelicals/whatitmeans.html.

10. Reemergent neo-orthodoxy is occurring in the emergent church movement. A prime example of this is found in Brian McLaren's, *A Generous Orthodox*, Youth Specialties: El Cajon, CA, 2004; published by Zondervan, p. 164, 165. Professor Jeffrey Jue, assistant professor of church history at Westminster Theological Seminary, does a superb job of connecting these dots

in his article, "What is the Emerging Church?" *Reformation*, 21, September 2005. This journal is available online at http://www.reformation21.org/1/.

11. Millard J. Erickson, *Reclaiming the Center* (Wheaton: Crossway, 2004), 324.

12. For a thorough treatment and explanation of postmodernism, I suggest Gary Aylesworth, "Postmodernism," *The Stanford Encyclopedia of Philosophy* (Winter 2005 Edition), Edward N. Zalta (ed.), http://plato.stanford.edu/archives/win2005/entries/postmodernism/. I would also suggest Mark Tabb, *Mission to Oz* (Chicago: Moody), 2004.

13. Donald Miller, *Blue Like Jazz* (Nashville: Thomas Nelson, 2003), 103.

14. Stanley Grenz, *Participating in What Frees: The Concept of Truth in the Postmodern Context*, *Review and Expositor* 100/4 (Fall 2003): 691.

15. Francis Schaeffer, *Escape from Reason* in *The Francis A. Schaeffer Trilogy* (Westchester, IL: Crossway, 1990), 43–65.

16. Ministry leaders who embrace the "proclamation model" of ministry stress the centrality of preaching as the dominant ministry of the local church. Preaching is the focal point of the worship service and is the primary task of the pastor. Proclamation churches have a very high regard for the authority of the Bible and believe that real life change is connected with hearing and responding to the Word of God as it is preached. The parish model sees the primary role of the pastor as pastoral care of people in their daily lives. The ministry is often one of counseling, visiting the sick, performing baptisms, weddings, and funerals, and meeting the needs of the poor. Parish ministries tend to view the surrounding community as part of the church whether or not a person attends the weekly service.

17. Roderick M. Chisholm, *Theory of Knowledge*, 3rd ed., *Foundations of Philosophy Series* (Englewood Cliffs, NJ: Prentice Hall, 1989), 16.

CHAPTER 5

1. Accessed at http://www.costcoconnection.com/connection/200408/.

2. Patricia Sullivan, "Management Visionary Peter Drucker Dies," *Washington Post*, November 12, 2005: B06.

3. The Drucker Foundation, *The Leader of the Future* (San Francisco: Jossey-Bass, 1996), 2.

4. Robert K. Greenleaf, *Servant Leadership* (New York: Paulist Press, 1977), 7–48.

5. Dennis Bakke, *Joy at Work* (Seattle: WA: PVG, 2005), 132–133.

6. Warren S. Bennis, *On Becoming a Leader* (Reading, MA: Addison-Wesley Publishing, 1989), 39–41.

7. Peter Block, *Stewardship* (San Francisco: Berret-Koehler, 1993), 3–22.

8. Stephen R. Covey, *Principle-Centered Leadership* (New York: Simon & Schuster, 1991), 33–39.

9. Max De Pree, *Leadership Is an Art* (New York: Dell, 1989), 11–22.

10. James M. Kouzes and Barry Z. Posner, *Encouraging the Heart: A Leader's Guide to Rewarding and Recognizing Others* (San Francisco: Jossey-Bass, 1999), 17.

11. Parker J. Palmer, *Let Your Life Speak: Listening to the Voice of Vocation* (San Francisco: Jossey-Bass, 2000), 73–94.

12. Tom Peters, *Liberation Management* (New York: Fawcett Columbine, 1992), 468–476.

13. Peter Senge, *The Fifth Discipline* (New York: Currency Doubleday, 1990) 339–362.

14. Dan Quayle, "Family Values are Key to Transforming the Underclass," Article in the *San Diego Union*, May 31, 1992, C-5.

15. Dan Quayle, *Standing Firm: A Vice Presidential Memoir* (New York: Harper Collins, 1994), 319–20.

16. Margaret Thatcher, speech given to the Glasgow Chamber of Commerce, February 28, 1983, at the Holiday Inn, Glasgow, Scotland.

17. From radio transcript IRN program *The Decision Makers,* broadcast at 11:00 a.m., Friday, April 15, 1983.

18. Dr. Martin Luther King Jr., *Stride Toward Freedom*, Reprint ed. (New York: Harper Collins Children's Books: January, 1987), 83.

19. Speech to the House of Commons, June 4, 1940.

20. Jon Meacham, *Franklin and Winston: An Intimate Portrait of an Epic Friendship* (New York: Random House, 2003), 367.

21. Harold Myra and Marshall Shelley, *The Leadership Secrets of Billy Graham* (Grand Rapids: Zondervan, 2005), 63.

22. Calvin's Commentary on 1 Timothy 3.2, http://www.ccel.org /c/calvin/comment3 /comm_vol43/htm/iii.v.htm.

23. Terry Pearce, *Leading Out Loud* (San Francisco: Jossey-Bass, 2003), 74.

24. Robert Galford and Anne Drapeau, *The Trusted Leader* (New York: The Free Press, 2002), 29–42.

25. J. Oswald Sanders, *Spiritual Leadership* (Chicago: Moody, 1994), 56.

26. Warren G. Bennis and Robert T. Thomas, "Crucibles of Leadership," *Harvard Business Review*, September 2002.

27. James E. Means, *Leadership in Christian Ministry* (Grand Rapids: Baker Books, 1989), 36.

28. "The Peace Prayer of St. Francis," http://www.franciscan-archive.org/index2.html.

29. Robert D. Putnam, *Bowling Alone: The Collapse and Revival of American Community* (New York: Touchstone Books, 2000), 135.

30. Anton C. Pegis, ed., *Introduction to St. Thomas Aquinas* (New York: The Modern Library, 1948), 588.

CHAPTER 6

1. http://away.com/primedia/military/fredericksburg_2.html.

2. Ibid.

3. http://www.historyplace.com/civilwar/index.html.

4. "Competency" as defined by *The American Heritage Dictionary of the English Language, Fourth Edition*, Houghton Mifflin Company, 2000.

5. Noel M. Tichy, *The Cycle of Leadership: How Great Leaders Teach Their Companies to Win* (New York: Harper Business, 2002), 74.

6. Ibid.

7. Haddon W. Robinson, *Biblical Preaching* (Grand Rapids: Baker Books, 1980), 31–48.

8. Gary Bredfeldt and Lawrence Richards, *Creative Bible Teaching* (Chicago: Moody, 1998) 61–73.

9. Retold from Terry Pearce, *Leading Out Loud* (San Francisco: Jossey-Bass, 2003), 55.

10. Bredfeldt and Richards, *Creative Bible Teaching,* 181–208.

11. Joanne Martin and Melanie Power, "Organizational Stories: More Vivid and Persuasive than Quantitative Data," *Psychological Foundations of Organizational Behavior*, ed. B. M. Staw (Glenview, IL: Scott Foresman, 1982), 161–168.

12. C. C. Bonwell and J. A. Eison, "Active Learning: Creating Excitement in the Classroom,"

NOTES

ASHE-ERIC Higher Education Report No. 1, George Washington University, School of Education and Human Development, Washington, DC, 1991.

13. James M. Kouzes and Barry Z. Posner, *The Leadership Challenge, 3rd Ed.* (San Francisco: Jossey-Bass, 2000), 43-108.

14. William J. Bennett, *Virtues of Leadership* (Nashville: Thomas Nelson, 2001), 6–8.

15. Jim Collins, *Good to Great* (New York: HarperCollins, 2001), 41–90.

16. Eddie Gibbs, *LeadershipNext: Changing Leaders in a Changing Culture* (Downers Grove, IL: InterVarsity, 2005), 43.

17. Ibid.

18. James M. Kouzes and Barry Z. Posner, *Encouraging the Heart* (San Francisco: Jossey-Bass, 1999), 15–31.

19. H. W. Croker III, *Robert E. Lee on Leadership* (Roseville, CA: Prema Publishing, 1999), 19–20.

20. Ibid, 159.

CHAPTER 7

1. John P. Kotter, *Leading Change* (Boston: Harvard Business School Press, 1996).

2. James O'Toole, *Leading Change* (New York: Ballantine Books), 1996.

3. Paul Hersey and Kenneth Blanchard, *Management of Organizational Behavior* (Englewood Cliffs, NJ: Prentice-Hall, 1993), 171–203.

4. Frederick Taylor, *The Principles of Scientific Management* (New York: Harper and Row, 1913), 9–29.

5. Henri Fayol, *General and Industrial Management* (London: Pitman, 1949), 19–42.

6. Aristotle, *A Treatise on Government*, trans. William Ellis, ed. Ernest Rhys (London: Dent and Sons, 1990), 226–227. See also Aristotle, *Politics, Book I, in Introduction to Aristotle* trans. Benjamin Jowett, ed. Richard McKeon (New York: Random House, 1947).

7. Warren Bennis and Burt Nanus, *Leaders* (New York: Harper Perennial, Harper Collins Publishers, 1986), 20.

8. Shelley A. Kirkpatrick and Edwin A. Locke, "Leadership: Do Traits Matter?" *Academy of Management Executive*, 5 (1991), 48–60.

CHAPTER 8

1. http://www.pbs.org/wgbh/nova/sciencenow/3204/02-knowthat.html.

2. Bernard Ramm, B. "The Holy Alliance," *His*, 1974, 34 (5), 12–15.

3. Mary Stewart Van Leeuwen, "Cognitive Style, North American Values and the Body of Christ," from *JASA* 27 (September 1975): 119–126. Paper presented at the Christian Association for Psychological Studies, Atlanta, Georgia, in April, 1974, and published in *Journal of Psychology and Theology* 2, 77 (1974).

4. Bernard Ramm, "The Way of the Spirit," *His*, 1974, 34 (6), 16–18, 22.

5. Rick Warren, *The Purpose-Driven Church* (Grand Rapids: Zondervan, 1995) 95–119.

6. Lawrence O. Richards and Clyde Hoeldtke, *A Theology of Church Leadership* (Grand Rapids: Zondervan, 1980), 62.

7. This sentiment was strongly expressed in a document entitled "The Word Made Fresh: A Call for a Renewal of the Evangelical Spirit." It can be read at http://jmm.aaa.net.au/articles/14234.htm.

8. Thom Rainer, *Breakout Churches: Discover How to Make the Leap* (Grand Rapids: Zondervan, 2005).

9. Luisa Kroll, "Christian Capitalism: Megachurches, Megabusinesses," Forbes.com. 9/17/03. Available at http://www.forbes.com/2003/09/17/cz_lk_0917megachurch.html.

10. Rick Warren, *The Purpose-Driven Church* (Grand Rapids: Zondervan, 1995). Bill Hybels, *Becoming a Contagious Christian* (Grand Rapids: Zondervan, 1996).

11. Daniel L. Akin, president, Southeastern Baptist Theological Seminary, Wake Forest, NC. "A 1st Century Vision for the 21st Century Church," delivered at Southern Baptist Theological Seminary, Mullin Lectures, 10/4/2005. Available for download online at http://www.sbts.edu/resources/audio/Fall2005.php.

CHAPTER 9

1. Account based on research material from the following books: J. M. G. Itard, *The Wild Boy of Aveyron* (1962). H. Lane, *The Wild Boy of Aveyron* (Englewood Cliffs, NJ: Prentice Hall, 1979). Roger Shattuck, *The Forbidden Experiment: The Story of the Wild Boy of Aveyron*, New York: Kodansha, 1994). M. Montessori, *The Secret of Childhood* (Notre Dame, IN: Fides Publishers, 1966).

2. James Means, *Leadership in Christian Ministry* (Grand Rapids: Baker Books, 1989), 111.

3. R. Albert Mohler, February 16, 2005, blog entry at Crosswalk.com. Mohler's entry can be read in its entirety at http://www.crosswalk.com/news/weblogs/mohler/?cal=go&adate=2%2F16%2F2005.

4. Ibid.

5. Transcribed from an NPR radio program. Though the comments are verbatim from the broadcast transcript and are exactly as spoken, I have intentionally changed the name of this person out of respect for privacy.

6. "Authentic" as defined by http://www.dictionary.com.

7. I have withheld the name of this researcher for a good reason. Christian people tend to react straightaway, usually negatively, when his name is mentioned. I am referring to Sigmund Freud. While I am no fan of Freud and do not accept the worldview presuppositions he embraces or his theory of human personality, his research in this area is both enlightening and helpful. I would encourage the reader to not discard everything Freud has theorized without giving due consideration to his research. Of course, let Scripture be your guide here as you discern truth from error.

8. Michael Maccoby, "Narcissistic Leaders: The Incredible Pros, the Inevitable Cons," *The Harvard Business Review*, January–February, 2000.

9. James Means, *Leadership in Christian Ministry* (Grand Rapids: Baker Books, 1989), 105.

10. Ibid., 105–106.

11. Taxonomy from J. French & B. H. Raven, *Studies of Social Power*, Institute for Social Research (Ann Arbor, MI, 1959).

12. Descriptions from Gary A. Yukl, *Leadership in Organizations*, Second ed., (New York: Prentice Hall, 1989), 34–53.

13. "Integrity" as defined by dictionary.com using *The American Heritage Dictionary of the English Language, Fourth Edition* (Chicago: Houghton Mifflin Company, 2000).

14. http://www.ewtn.com/library/MARY/DELASALL.htm, article taken from *The Saints: A Concise Biographical Dictionary*, John Coulson, ed. (Hawthorn Books, Inc., 1960).